Living In Light Of The Manger

A 40-Day Christmas Advent

Sheila Alewine
Around The Corner Ministries

www.aroundthecornerministries.org

Around The Corner Ministries exists to take the gospel to every neighborhood in America. Our mission is to equip followers of Jesus to engage their neighborhoods and communities with the gospel of Jesus Christ.

© 2017 by Sheila Alewine

ISBN: 978-0-9991318-1-7

Scripture quotations taken from the New American Standard Bible® (NASB), Copyright © 1960, 1962, 1963, 1968, 1971, 1972, 1973, 1975, 1977, 1995 by The Lockman Foundation. Used by permission. www.Lockman.org.

Introduction

What does Christmas really mean to you? It's become wholly commercialized, with decorations appearing on store shelves right next to the Halloween costumes and Thanksgiving paper plates. Black Friday now starts before the turkey and dressing leftovers have been stored in the fridge, enticing us to shop early to get those Christmas lists covered at the best possible price.

What if there's more? What if we really believed the story about a baby in a manger, a bright, shining star, angels appearing to shepherds, and wise men bringing gifts? What if Christmas is actually good news that can change our life?

Our fascination and longing for Christmas begins as a child, irrespective if we were taught the story of Christ's birth or were only given the Santa Claus version. One thing is certain – Christmas is about giving. Whether it's the local Angel Tree, ringing a bell beside a Salvation Army bucket, or volunteering at the soup kitchen, there's a draw on our heart to give back, give out, and give up our time and money when the calendar approaches December 25th. And it's only natural – for Christmas truly is about a gift.

You hold in your hands the opportunity to discover the truth about Christmas. Maybe you're very familiar with this story, and already believe it to be true. This journey towards Christmas will refresh your heart in the power of the gospel, reminding you of the miracle of new life in Christ – the gift Jesus has given you.

But if you're still thinking that Christmas is just about family celebrations and time off from work, and that giving is only about the presents under the tree, I invite you to stop and ponder for the next forty days. Open your heart and your mind to consider the powerful, life-changing, eternal truths of why God sent a baby to redeem the world. Open your heart to learn what it means to **live in light of the manger.**

***

Note: This devotional is designed to cause us to reflect on the meaning of Christmas. A 40-day Advent journey would begin on November 16 and end on December 25. Optionally, you could begin your reading on December 5 and two devotions each day – a morning and evening reflection.

Contents

The Purpose of the Manger
Day 1 – Day 3

*Now all these things are from God, who reconciles us to Himself
through Christ and gave us the ministry of reconciliation,
namely, that God was in Christ reconciling the world to Himself,
not counting their trespasses against them,
and He has committed to us the word of reconciliation.*
2 Corinthians 5:18-19

What does it mean to "live in light of the manger?"
It is to see the manger for what it truly represents. It is to ask ourselves the
question, "Why?" And when we discover the "why" we must respond.
The manger only makes sense if it has a purpose – a reason for its
appearance in the history of mankind.

Why did Jesus come?
Why was the Son of God born as a human baby?

To discover the answer, we must go all the way back to the beginning.
We go back to Creation.

Take It In

Then God said, "Let Us make man in Our image, according to Our likeness; and let them rule over the fish of the sea and over the birds of the sky and over the cattle and over all the earth, and over every creeping thing that creeps on the earth." God created man in His own image, in the image of God He created him, male and female He created them. ... God saw all that He had made, and behold, it was very good. And there was evening and there was morning, the sixth day. (Genesis 1:26-27, 31)

Think It Through

Why Christmas? From the world's perspective, Christmas is simply another holiday borne out of religious tradition, and the meaning behind it is pretty well obscured. And even for believers, it often becomes a frantic season of spending our time, money and energy on things that have little to do with the real reason we celebrate this special day.

We celebrate Christmas as the birthday of Jesus, but the reality is that Jesus doesn't have a birthday. Jesus existed in eternity past, and was present and active in *our beginning* – creation. Notice the words, "Let Us make man." In the beginning, right there in the Garden of Eden, Adam and Eve were created perfect, in the image of God, and they enjoyed a holy relationship in sinless perfection with God the Father, Jesus the Son, and the Spirit of God. This was our original destiny, the reason God created us.

Christmas, and all it embraces – the gifts we buy, the food we prepare, the parties we plan, the family gatherings we attend, and even the special services at our places of worship – all are meaningless unless we understand the real reason Jesus entered our world. Jesus stepped out of eternity and into our world to restore us to that perfect relationship we were created to enjoy with God.

Live It Out

What do you think of when you see a tiny baby in a manger? If we just see Christmas as the beginning of Jesus' life, we miss the real reason He was born. The manger calls us to remember *our beginning*, and to contemplate the magnificent truth that Jesus came to restore us and reconcile us to His Father. Only then does Christmas make sense, and can truly be celebrated.

Colossians 1:15-16 – *He [Jesus] is the image of the invisible God, the firstborn of all creation. For by Him all things were created, both in the heavens and on earth, visible and invisible, whether thrones or dominions or rulers or authorities – all things have been created through Him and for Him.*

PRAY TODAY
Dear Jesus, Today I worship You as my Creator. I recognize that You did not begin Your life when You entered my world as a human baby, but that You existed in eternity past, and were present in the Garden when Adam and Eve were created. You created us, because You desired a relationship with human men and women – a relationship of sinless perfection. Thank You for never giving up on us, and for Your willingness to come to our world and live as a human so that we could be reconciled to You. Help me to worship You this Christmas season, not just as the baby in the manger, but as Creator God, who loved me and desired me. Amen.

Day Two

Take It In
Then the Lord God formed man of dust from the ground, and breathed into his nostrils the breath of life; and man became a living being. (Genesis 2:7)

Think It Through
What did *our beginning* look like? When we say the manger speaks of our restoration, to what are we referring?

God created man from the dust of the earth, and breathed into him – the very breath of God gave **life** to Adam. He stood up from the ground and the first face He saw was His Creator. We don't know how God appeared to Adam in those first days of life, but we know they communicated in a very special, personal way. Genesis 3:8 refers to God's habit of walking in the garden in the cool of the day – coming to meet and spend time with these two beautiful creatures He had intimately fashioned for Himself to enjoy. *In the beginning, we had perfect communion with God, our spirit alive to Him.*

God so loved Adam that He wanted him to have a helper, another of his own kind to live with. So, He created Eve from Adam's rib – bone of his bone, and flesh of his flesh. God gave them to one another, and they became one flesh, unashamed, innocent. *In the beginning, we were sinless, and enjoyed perfect relationships with each other.*

9

God also provided for Adam and Eve's physical needs. He placed them in the garden, to cultivate it. This beautiful place provided their food to eat; their work was simple, uncomplicated, and unhindered by thorns or weeds. Their only task was to enjoy God's garden and His fellowship. *In the beginning, we had a perfect purpose, to enjoy God and the world He had provided.*

Live It Out

The manger was not Jesus' first visit to our world. In the beginning, He walked in the cool of the day, communing with Adam and Eve, helping them discover the beautiful world He had made for them. He could enjoy their presence, as they were sinless, perfect. He taught them how to care for the garden, and the animals that filled the fields and mountains, seas, and sky. They worshipped God in perfect holiness.

In the garden, God gave Adam and Eve life. And in the manger, Jesus came to give life again. He came as the breath of God, to the people He had created, to restore us to the perfect communion, the perfect relationships, and the perfect purpose we once had.

Today, think about how God has restored you. Are you in communion with Him and others, living out the purpose for which He created you? Restoration is available to all, but only through Jesus.

Jesus said to him, "I am the way, and the truth, and the life; no one comes to the Father but through Me." (John 14:6)

PRAY TODAY
Dear Jesus, I am envious when I read in Your word of what Adam and Eve enjoyed with You in the garden. To be in perfect relationship with You, in a perfect world with no sin, no hurt, no pain – to experience what You created us for – that is the longing of all our hearts. Thank You for the manger, that it reminds me that You came to restore. You desired us even when we rejected You. You came to give us life again – to breathe into our souls the breath of life. Thank You for loving us that much. Amen.

Day Three

Take It In

The serpent said to the woman, you surely will not die! For God knows that in the day you eat from it your eyes will be opened, and you will be like God, knowing good and evil." When the woman saw that the tree was good for food, and that it was a delight to the eyes, and that the tree was desirable to make one wise, she took from its fruit and ate; and she gave also to her husband with her, and he ate. Then the eyes of them both were opened, and they knew that they were naked; and they sewed fig leaves together and made themselves loin coverings. (Genesis 3:4-7)

Think It Through

How many times have we made a decision, only to instantly regret it? We've all experienced that drop in the pit of our stomach the moment we do or say something, knowing our decision has cost us something precious. I am quite sure that Eve felt this the moment she bit into the piece of fruit from the tree, and not knowing what to do, turned and handed it to Adam to join her in stepping across the line of God's only restriction. None of us want to take full responsibility for our foolish decisions!

In these four short verses, which changed the course of man's destiny, there is a principle at work – temptation. How did the serpent (the devil) instigate the sin?

First, he offered a false promise: *You surely will not die!*
Second, he offered a false position: *You will be like God!*
Third, he offered a false knowledge: *You will know good and evil!*

We know the serpent lied, because of the consequences: Adam and Eve died physically, and their spiritual life – their connection to God – was broken. Instead of becoming like God and able to discern good and evil, each generation after them would lose more and more of its ability to discern, becoming evil continually (Genesis 6, Romans 1).

Live It Out

In stark contrast, the manger tells us a different story. Jesus came to rewrite our destiny. Instead of temptation, the manger tells us the truth.

Only Jesus tells us the truth about death – by coming to die in our place.

Only Jesus shows us what God is like – by becoming Emmanuel, God with us.

Only Jesus gives us knowledge of good and evil – by sending His Spirit to indwell those who believe.

Consider who you are listening to. Are you believing the whispered lies of the serpent, or the truth that calls from the manger? We all have a tree in the middle of our garden. What decision will you make?

John 1:14 - *And the Word became flesh, and dwelt among us, and we saw His glory, glory as of the only begotten from the Father, full of grace and truth.*

PRAY TODAY

Dear Jesus, Thank You for the truth that speaks from the manger. The very fact that You came into this world shows us we had a need we couldn't fix. When Adam and Eve sinned, something precious was broken – our relationship with You. Help me to recognize the lies that deceive me, and keep me from understanding Your truth, and the real message of the manger. Open my eyes to see who You are, and give me a heart that is willing to accept the truth about my own sin, and what You did to fix it. Amen.

The Promise of the Manger
Day 4 – Day 7

From the descendants of this man [David], according to promise,
God has brought to Israel a Savior, Jesus.
And we preach to you the good news of the promise
made to the fathers, that God has fulfilled this promise
to our children in that He raised up Jesus, as it is also written
in the second Psalm, "You are My Son; today I have begotten You."
Acts 13:23,32-33

The purpose of the manger is our restoration;
a return to our former place in God's perfect kingdom and to be reconciled
to God. But the purpose was not achieved quickly. For many years, God
made promises to His people, that a Messiah would come – One who would
set right what had been made wrong.

The promise also began in the garden. In the middle of the worst
day of their life, Adam and Eve received the best news:
the promise of the manger.

Take It In

The Lord God said to the serpent..."And I will put enmity between you and the woman, and between your seed and her seed; He shall bruise you on the head and you shall bruise him on the heel." (Genesis 3:15)

Think It Through

Here we see the very first promise in Scripture that would lead to the manger. Adam and Eve had sinned, breaking the perfect relationship between God and humanity. Their decision to disobey God's command not to eat of the tree of knowledge of good and evil was costly. They lost their place (the garden), their position (intimate fellowship with the Creator), and their perfection (sin now ruled in their flesh). More than that, their sin brought death – both physical (separation from this life) and spiritual (separation from God for eternity).

In Genesis 3:15, however, God makes a promise. The seed of the woman would bruise the serpent (the devil) on the head, destroying his position and power. Who is this seed? It is Jesus, the baby in the manger.

The word "advent" means "a coming into place, view or being; an arrival." The advent of Jesus did not begin when the angel visited Mary, or when the Holy Spirit implanted God incarnate in her womb. The advent of Jesus starts here, in the garden, spoken to Adam and Eve in their separation and brokenness. Standing before a holy God, fully exposed in their sin, they hear the promise of a Savior, who would be born, so that they could be born again.

Live It Out

At some point in our life, we all stand before God, exposed in our sin. Has this happened to you? Have you realized your separation from the Creator God, the One who made you and placed you in your garden, the world you live in? If you have, the manger speaks of the good news that Jesus was born, so that you could be born again.

As we begin this Advent season, a celebration of the arrival of Jesus into world, examine your heart. Is there any sin that needs to be confronted or exposed? The manger calls us to remember that first conflict in the garden as God called Adam and Eve to confront their sin. It calls us to prepare our hearts to worship the baby who is coming. And in the examining, remember the promise that sin's power would be broken, through the seed of the woman – Jesus.

1 Timothy 1:15 – *It is a trustworthy statement, deserving full acceptance, that Christ Jesus came into the world to save sinners, among whom I am foremost of all.*

PRAY TODAY

Dear Jesus, As I begin this season of advent, turning my heart and my mind to ponder the wonder of your birth, I ask You to examine me. I want to come before You in holiness, because You are worthy to be worshipped. Thank You for confronting me, showing me my sin, just like you did for Adam and Eve in the garden. And thank You for the promise of Jesus, who came to heal us of our sinfulness, and break sin's power in our life. Amen.

Day Five

Take It In

Therefore the Lord God sent him [Adam] out from the garden of Eden, to cultivate the ground from which he was taken. So He drove the man out; and at the east of the garden of Eden He stationed the cherubim and the flaming sword which turned every direction to guard the way to the tree of life. (Genesis 3:24)

Think It Through

Have you ever looked back to your ancestors' history and wished that you could change some things they did, that are still affecting you today? Today, for less than $100, you can send off a sample of your saliva and have your DNA tested to discover your ethnicity (where your ancestors lived) and even be connected to strangers who are related to you! The technology is amazing, but it shouldn't surprise us to know that we are all related to one another at some point in our genealogy. After all, *we are all related to Adam and Eve!*

While we may be delighted to know that our brown eyes come from our great grandfather, and our love of jazz reflects a great aunt with a similar talent for music, there's one thing we inherited that we can't deny...our sin nature. When Adam and Eve sinned, their perfect human nature was defiled. They had been created *in the likeness (image) of God.* In contrast, their children were born *in their own likeness, according to Adam's image.* (Genesis 5:1-3.)

The consequences that Adam and Eve suffered from their sin, a removal from the garden of Eden and the denial of access to the tree of life are now our consequences. We are banished from God's presence, and have no access to eternal life. Their sin brought death, and because we now all sin (Romans 3:23), we all die. This is our inheritance.

Live It Out

You may be thinking, that's not fair. Why should we suffer for what someone else did? And I would agree with you. But here are two thoughts to consider.

First, God is just. It is in His DNA, and He cannot deny Himself. In His justness, He could not condemn an innocent soul. But as Romans 5:12 and 3:23 says, all have sinned. 2 Samuel 12:23 indicates there is a grace for babies, who do not yet have the consciousness of sin, but the fact is, *we have all sinned*, and we are all guilty, not just by inheritance, but by our behavior.

Second, God understands what it means to suffer for someone else's actions. Isn't that the message of the manger? Jesus came into our world as the only perfect, sinless One who lived a perfect, sinless human life. For what reason? To become the One who would hang on a cross for *someone else's actions*...your sin, and my sin.

Have you faced the certainty of your own personal sin? The reality is, we inherited something we don't want, and we don't need a DNA test to tell us it's there. We can look at our own heart and see what separates us from the God who loves us. But I'm so thankful we can look at the manger and see the solution – Jesus!

Romans 5:12 – *Therefore, just as through one man sin entered into the world, and death through sin, and so death spread to all men, because all sinned.*

PRAY TODAY

Dear Jesus, Sometimes I wish that we could rewind history and allow Adam and Eve a "do-over." I'm hopeful that they would make a better decision. But I know in my heart that sin's temptation is strong, and that if Adam and Eve didn't sin, their children or grandchildren would, because You graciously gave us a free will, and in our humanity, we want to go our own way, even when we have everything we need in You. Thank You for your grace and mercy that You provided a solution for our sin in Jesus. Help me to recognize my own sin, not to dwell on its ugliness or regret, but to see how great Your salvation is. Thank You for not doing what was "fair" for You, but what was necessary for me. Amen.

Take It In

The Lord God made garments of skin for Adam and his wife, and clothed them. (Genesis 3:21)

Think It Through

This little verse might be one you just skip right over. After all, it doesn't sound like anything deep or profound. We know that in their original, perfect state of being, Adam and Eve were naked, unashamed. It makes sense that when God sent them out of the garden into the world to work and strive for their livelihood, He made them clothes. It seems a trivial detail, doesn't it?

Here's a lesson for us: everything God tells us in His Word is significant.

When Adam and Eve sinned, their first response was to *hide*. Genesis 2:7-8 tells us they suddenly knew they were naked, so they sewed fig leaves to cover themselves, and hid among the trees from the presence of God. This is our natural response to realizing we have sinned. Something within us makes us aware of our unworthiness before God: we are guilty. You might call it your conscience, but I believe it is because we are created in the image of God for the purpose of worshipping our Creator, and we know when have broken His law.

The way that Adam and Eve tried *to cover* their sin illustrates our inability to change our sinful state. Fig leaves are temporary, fragile. They would last for a little while, but soon they would wilt and tear, leaving them exposed once again. Do you find it interesting that they tried to use what God had given them for beauty and provision to make up for their sin? Think about that.

Live It Out

What was God's answer to cover their guilt? He made them garments of skin. Something had to die. A sacrifice had to be made. An innocent animal lost its life to provide a covering for their sinfulness. Notice two things:

God made the garments. He performed the sacrifice.
God clothed them. He covered their sinfulness Himself.

God's actions in the garden are a picture of what He would do on the cross thousands of years later. The garments of skin are a promise, that one day, a baby would be born, sent from heaven to live a perfect life and become the ultimate sacrifice that would cover the sins of all mankind, forever.

As you look at that baby in the manger, consider why He came. Remember the picture of our gracious and merciful Father, gently placing garments of skin around His beloved creation who had sinned against Him, as a promise of a better and final covering for our sin.

John 1:29 – *The next day he [John the Baptist] saw Jesus coming to him, and said, "Behold, the Lamb of God, who takes away the sin of the world!"*

PRAY TODAY
Dear Jesus, Thank You that nothing in Your word is insignificant. You have so much You want us to understand. Remind us to always stop and think about the meaning of Your words, even ones that seem trivial. You made a sacrifice to cover the first sins of Your beloved creation, and You made the ultimate sacrifice when You came to this world as a baby, to die on a cross for all our sin. You covered Adam & Even with temporary garments of skin, and You cover us with the righteousness of Christ. As I ponder the miracle of Your birth this today, help me not to forget the real reason You came. Amen.

Day Seven

Take It In
For a child will be born to us, a son will be given to us; and the government will rest on His shoulders; and His name will be called Wonderful Counselor, Mighty God, Eternal Father, Prince of Peace. There will be no end to the increase of His government or of peace, on the throne of David and over his kingdom, to establish it and to uphold it with justice and righteousness from then on and forevermore. The zeal of the Lord of hosts will accomplish this. (Isaiah 9:6-7)

Think It Through
When this verse in Isaiah was written, several thousand years had passed since Adam and Eve were banished from the garden. During that time, God formed the nation of Israel, selecting Abraham and Sarah as the beginning of His chosen people. He created a people through which He would send His Son, Jesus as the promised Messiah.

The nation of Israel went through a tumultuous and colorful history: times of slavery, war, famine, drought, and wilderness wanderings. They were fickle children of God – one generation would serve Him faithfully, and the next would turn away to false gods. God rescued them time after time, performing miracles in their midst. He revealed Himself to them through His law and His prophets, shaping them into a unique culture. He also revealed Himself through the Word, as He spoke through the men who recorded history and prophesied of the promise of a Savior.

The Jewish people had no doubts that a Messiah was coming. More than 300 prophecies are recognized in Scripture that refer to the One who would fulfill God's promise. Isaiah 9:6-7 is only one. Statistically, the odds of fulfilling just eight prophecies would be 1 in 100,000,000,000,000,000! To fulfill 48 prophecies would be 1 in 10 to the 157th power! The odds of a person fulfilling 300+ prophecies cannot be expressed...and only Jesus did it.

Live It Out

What do statistics have to do with a tiny baby in a manger? Is it important to know that Jesus fulfilled prophecies made over the span of generations – by men who had no knowledge of each other, and nothing to gain by making them up?

The prophecies are important because they confirm the truth of the message God is telling throughout the Bible – the message of redemption. The story of man began in a garden, and as God weaves the timeline of history, He has one overarching purpose and plan: to reclaim His creation through the miracle of salvation in Jesus, by faith, through grace.

Do you believe that the baby in the manger is the promised One? That He came to save His people from their sins? Recognizing we are sinful and separated from God is the first step to salvation. Recognizing Jesus as the Savior is the next. The manger holds not just another baby, but the hope for our eternity. Do you believe?

Luke 24:44-45 – *Now He [Jesus] said to them, "These are My words which I spoke to you while I was still with you, that all things which are written about Me in the Law of Moses and the Prophets and the Psalms must be fulfilled." Then He opened their minds to understand the Scriptures.*

PRAY TODAY

Dear Jesus, I recognize You as the promised One that all the Old Testament prophets wrote about. You were not just a good man, or another prophet, but You are the promised Son of God who came to rescue us from our sins and restore us to Your Father. When I look at You as the baby in the manger, I see the fulfillment of all that God promised to do to redeem us. Thank You for giving us confidence in who You are through Your word. Amen.

The Presence of the Manger
Day 8 – Day 13

Jesus said to him, "Because you have seen Me, have you believed?
Blessed are they who did not see, and yet believed.
Therefore many other signs Jesus also performed in the
presence of the disciples, which are not written in this book;
but these have been written so that you may believe
that Jesus is the Christ, the Son of God; and that believing
You may have life in His name.
John 20:29-31

Mary and Joseph knew that a Messiah had been promised. But they never
expected that the promise would become a presence in their life!
We envy Mary and Joseph, and wonder if we would find it
easier to believe if we experienced the manger as they did.

But the fact is, the manger's presence affects us all.
It speaks of God's favor, His blessing, and His commands.
It changes us. It challenges us.
And it stands before us, calling us to believe.

Take It In

Now in the sixth month the angel Gabriel was sent from God to a city in Galilee called Nazareth, to a virgin engaged to a man whose name was Joseph, of descendants of David; and the virgin's name was Mary. And coming in, he said to her, "Greetings, favored one! The Lord is with you." But she was very perplexed at this statement, and kept pondering what kind of salutation this was. The angel said to her, "Do not be afraid, Mary; for you have found favor with God. And behold, you will conceive in your womb and bear a son, and you shall name Him Jesus." (Luke 1:26-31)

Think It Through

Put yourself in Mary's place. Her life seems to be going in a perfectly normal direction. She is engaged to a Jewish man, a legally binding time of waiting until marriage. She sees herself living out her life as expected, the simple life of a Jewish wife, raising her children and creating a home with her husband. In the time it takes to have a short conversation with a visiting angel, her world is turned upside down!

The angel refers to Mary as a "favored one." The phrase in the Greek means to endue or pursue with grace, to compass with favor, and to honor with blessings. What is the blessing or grace bestowed on Mary? Certainly, to be chosen to carry the very Son of God was a special blessing, but it would also cause her incredible pain and hardship, not only in the beginning of His life, as she faced the accusations of being an unwed mother, but also as she would stand at the foot of the cross and watch Him die.

The real grace and blessing bestowed on Mary is found in the angel's next phrase, "The Lord is with you." How do we know this? Consider his next words, "Do not be afraid, Mary, for you have found favor with God." The angel knew what God was asking of this young girl – to completely surrender her life to His sovereign purposes. He was asking her to turn away from all her plans for a simple, happy life, and risk everything to bring His Son into the world. But the grace...the favor...the blessing that would sustain her and calm her fears was the presence of God in her life: *the Lord is with you.*

Live It Out

The manger speaks of the presence of God in our lives as well – God has come to us. His very name, Immanuel, means *God with us.* Did you know that you are "highly favored" just as Mary was, because God has invited you into His grace, through faith in Christ?

The same Greek word used to address Mary as "favored" by God is found in Ephesians 1:6, referring to believers. Speaking of God's grace, Paul tells us that it has been "freely bestowed" on us. The KJV says it another way, that God has "made us accepted." To be accepted by God is to be highly favored, blessed, because in Christ, *the Lord is with us.*

How have you responded to God's offer of grace and favor? It *will* turn your life upside down, just as it did Mary's. It calls for a surrender of our plans for our life – a laying down of ourselves for His sovereign purposes. May our response be the same as Mary's.

Luke 1:38 – *And Mary said, "Behold, the bondslave of the Lord; may it be done to me according to your word."*

PRAY TODAY
Dear Jesus, Thank You for the example of Mary. You asked a lot of her – You turned her life upside down. But in calling her to be Your servant, You blessed her with Your presence. Help me to be willing to trust You with my life, because Your presence is worth far more than any plans I have. I want Your presence here in this life, and even more – I want to live in Your presence for eternity. Thank You for offering me the grace and acceptance found in salvation in You. Amen.

Day Nine

Take It In
Therefore the Lord Himself will give you a sign; Behold, a virgin will be with child and bear a son, and she will call His name Immanuel. (Isaiah 7:14)

Mary said to the angel, "How can this be, since I am a virgin?" (Luke 1:34)

Think It Through
The words of the prophet Isaiah were spoken 700 years before they were fulfilled. In the immediate context, they were given as a sign to the wicked king of Israel, Ahaz. Enemies were approaching Jerusalem, and through the prophet Isaiah, God tells him if he will believe, that He will save him, but if he chooses not to believe, he would not last. Isaiah tells the king to ask God for a sign, but in his stubbornness and refusal to believe in God's power to protect him, he refuses to ask for a sign, under the pretense of refusing to "test the Lord." You see, if he asked for a sign and it came true, then he would have to admit God was sovereignly alive and active in the world. He would have to believe.

Isaiah responds that "the Lord Himself will give you a sign." In other words, I will prove that I am who I say I am! I will demonstrate that I am the sovereign Lord over all creation – the one true God.

Both Matthew and Luke assure us that this prophecy is ultimately fulfilled in Christ, as He is born of a virgin, an unmarried young woman who has never known a man (Matthew 1:22-23). For Mary, she most certainly would have known about this prophecy, and would have realized that God had sovereignly chosen her for this role. By her humble response and willingness to serve, she demonstrated a true and honest belief in the sovereignty of God over her life.

Live It Out

The manger stands in front of us as a testimony of God's sovereignty. Its presence in Mary's life confirms that she was chosen by God, and that she believed in and surrendered to His sovereign plan.

But how about us? Are we chosen? Does God have a plan for our lives? Ephesians 1 tells us that we are chosen in Christ to become holy and blameless, to be adopted as sons of God, because of the kindness of His will. 2 Peter 3:9 tells us that He desires all to come to repentance. And Acts 17:26 tells us that God is sovereign even over the places we live and the time we are born!

Just as God had a sovereign plan for Mary's life – a role for her to fulfill in His great plan of the redemption of mankind – He also has a plan for you! What is our response? We have two choices. We can refuse to accept the sign and perish, as Ahaz did, or we can believe and humbly submit to the grace and love God offers, as we see in Mary's case. How have you responded?

Ephesians 1:4 – *Just as He chose us in Him before the foundation of the world, that we would be holy and blameless before Him.*

PRAY TODAY
Dear Jesus, I bow before Your sovereignty today. I trust You with my life, because I see in Jesus how much You love me. I believe that You have a plan for my life, and that Your plan begins with accepting Your offer of salvation. I want my life to fulfill the purposes that You have planned for me, and I submit myself humbly to Your sovereignty. Thank You for demonstrating Your sovereignty in Mary's life, so that I can understand more of You. Amen.

Take It In

The angel answered and said to her, "The Holy Spirit will come upon you, and the power of the Most High will overshadow you; and for that reason the holy Child shall be called the Son of God." (Luke 1:35)

Think It Through

The word "overshadow" means exactly what you think, to envelop in a shadow, and presents a beautiful picture of our God.

In the Old Testament, the presence of God is physically seen in the form of a cloud. Beginning in Exodus 13:21, we see God leading and protecting the children of Israel personally, in the cloud by day and the pillar of fire by night. This cloud, this visible manifestation, is the glory of God on the wilderness tabernacle, on the mountain where Moses received the ten commandments, and on Solomon's temple, assuring the people of His presence. Always, this was an outward, external sign.

In the New Testament, we encounter this word "overshadow" only five times, and in three contexts. First, here in Luke, describing the way that God planted the seed of His Son in Mary's womb. The second time is in the account of Jesus' transfiguration (Matthew 17:5, Mark 9:7, Luke 9:34). God's Spirit was a physical manifestation, an outward, external sign of His presence when Jesus' divine glory was revealed to Peter, James and John. The final appearance of the word is in reference to Peter's shadow, as having healing properties when it fell upon the sick (Acts 5:15).

So, we see God's presence, His Spirit, in the Old Testament as a cloud, moving from place to place to lead, guide, and protect externally, and in the New Testament as a cloud appearing for a specific purpose, overshadowing, acting from the outside, *except* in the case of Peter, where the power to heal came from within Peter, to fall on the sick!

What had happened to Peter to cause him to be a vessel of such power, which could only come from God? He had been indwelt by the Holy Spirit at Pentecost, fifty days after Jesus' resurrection (Acts 2)! No longer do we look for a visible cloud to follow, or assure us of God's presence, as an outward, external sign. The same Spirit of God that implanted Jesus in Mary's body now dwells within the believer and has given us new life in Christ!

Live It Out

Mary received the life of the Son of God physically within her womb, by the power of the Holy Spirit. As believers today, living on this side of the cross and resurrection, we receive the new life of that same indwelling Spirit, to empower us and assure us of Christ's presence.

The manger tells us that God has come to dwell in us. And the miracle of the indwelling Spirit assures us that our sins have been forgiven, and we are truly accepted by God, for God cannot dwell in sin. The next time you look at a cloud in the sky, remember the manger, where the glory of God came down, and thank Him for the salvation that enables Him to dwell in you.

1 John 4:13 - *By this we know that we abide in Him and He in us, because He has given us of His Spirit.*

PRAY TODAY
Dear Jesus, The miracle of Your physical birth through a virgin girl astounds us. Some would say it is impossible, but I know that all things are possible with You. And I know this because not only did Your Spirit place Your divine presence in Mary's womb, You also indwell us, as Your children. Your word assures us that when we turn away from our sin to follow You, that You will come in and dwell with us. Thank You for this miracle. Help me to live in such a way that others know that You live in me. Amen.

Day Eleven

Take It In
While they were there, the days were completed for her to give birth. And she gave birth to her first born son; and she wrapped Him in cloths, and laid Him in a manger, because there was no room for them in the inn. (Luke 2:6-7)

Think It Through
These familiar words are the heart of the nativity story that is played out by Christmas programs all over the world at this time of year. Bedsheets are styled into first century clothing, sanctuaries are staged with crude wooden mangers and hay from the nearest farm, and the youngest infant in the congregation is recruited to play the baby Jesus, hopefully to sleep through the singing of *Silent Night* and the noisy appearance of angels with tulle wings and glittered halos. It's a scene that stirs our heart no matter how young or old the players may be.

But also contained in these two short verses are theological truths that can change our destiny. Consider first that Jesus was born at a specific, sovereignly designated time: *the days were completed.* Not only the days of Mary's normal nine months of pregnancy, but at this particular point in history, at the very time Caesar Augustus would call for a census that would place Mary and Joseph in Bethlehem – the city prophesied for the Messiah's birth!

Note also that Jesus was born in humility – wrapped in cloths and laid in a manger. This was not the arrival "fit for a king" but rather for a simple, ordinary baby – and a poor one at that. And finally, look at their surroundings. They were (most likely) in a cave behind the inn, where the livestock were kept. We see this as though the city were unwelcoming, but in fact, the innkeeper went above and beyond to find a place for the Son of God to make His entrance. He opened the only door he had.

Live It Out

Let's unpack these three observations and consider if the manger's presence in the stable has any meaning for us. As we've said before, Jesus was born, so that we could be born again. As He passed from His world into ours, so we must pass from our old life apart from God, and be born anew into the kingdom of God (John 3:3 – *Jesus said...Unless one is born again, he cannot see the kingdom of God.*) And just like Jesus' arrival, our salvation must happen at a certain time and a certain place. It is a point in time when we spiritually and physically surrender our heart and life to God's conviction and call. It may be a quiet, inner laying down of self, or a dramatic and emotional affair – but new birth must happen at a point in time!

Secondly, Jesus' humble beginnings illustrate two points. We are born again in humility, a sign of repentance and turning away from our pride and self-working to achieve heaven; and this new birth is available to all, no matter your circumstances. Jesus came to a common, ordinary place to show that our status in life has no impact on our need (or lack of need) for a Savior. The heart of man is the same, and all must be humbled.

And finally, just as the innkeeper opened the door to the only place He could offer, so we must open the door to our heart – for it is all we have to give, and it is the only thing He asks. Have you opened the door?

Revelation 3:20 - *Behold, I stand at the door and knock; if anyone hears My voice and opens the door, I will come in to him and will dine with him, and he with Me.*

PRAY TODAY

Dear Jesus, I am so grateful that You were willing to leave heaven to be born in such humble circumstances. Your arrival was planned by our Sovereign Father at just the right time, in just the right place. In the same way, You speak to our heart, convicting and calling us to come to You at a certain time in our life, and we must respond. For those of us who have responded, thank You for the new life we receive from You. And for those who do not yet believe, keep calling, and give strength and faith to respond. Amen.

Day Twelve

Take It In

Now the birth of Jesus Christ was as follows: when His mother Mary had been betrothed to Joseph, before they came together she was found to be with child by the Holy Spirit. And Joseph, her husband, being a righteous man and not wanting to disgrace her, planned to send her away secretly. But when he had considered this, behold, an angel of the Lord appeared to him in a dream, saying, "Joseph, son of David, do not be afraid to take Mary as your wife; for the Child who has been conceived in her is of the Holy Spirit. She will bear a Son; and you shall call His name Jesus, for He will save His people from their sins."... And Joseph arose from his sleep and did as the angel of the Lord commanded him, and took Mary as his wife, but kept her a virgin until she gave birth to a Son; and he called His name Jesus. (Matthew 1:19-21, 24-25)

Think It Through

Joseph is one of my favorite characters in the story of Jesus' birth. We don't know much about him, other than he was a descendant of the tribe of Judah, in the line of David. He was a righteous man, and a carpenter, and we know that he truly loved Mary, seeing his desire not to make her a public example and disgrace her when she was found to be pregnant.

This interruption into his planned life would have obviously caused him concern, but I find it interesting that it didn't seem to keep him up at night! Perhaps because God spoke to him in his dreams (multiple times) he had not acquired the habit of worrying, but to simply lay down and wait for God to give him direction. He had learned the secret of Psalm 4:8, in which the psalmist says, *In peace I will both lie down and sleep, for You alone, O Lord, make me to dwell in safety.*

In describing Joseph, Matthew uses the word *dikaios*, translated "just" or "righteous." It describes one who keeps the commands of God. One definition reads this way: *Used of him whose way of thinking, feeling, and acting is wholly conformed to the will of God, and who therefore needs no rectification in the heart or life.* Only Christ is truly righteous, needing no change in heart or life, but the word describes a man whose heart and mind was committed to an attitude and lifestyle of obedient trust, no matter what God asked of him. Notice in Matthew 1:24, as soon as Joseph awoke from his dream, he immediately took steps to carry out God's plan, and married Mary. He had no hesitation, because his heart was already fully committed to obey. He simply needed the direction to go.

Live It Out

For Joseph, the presence of the manger in his life would call him again and again to trust and obey God. He withstood the skeptical criticism of his family and friends, to marry a pregnant fiancé. They would have assumed that he and Mary had sinned, or that he was foolishly being faithful to a promiscuous girl. His trust and obedience to God would be tested throughout the life of the Child, as God directed their steps to Egypt in protecting Him from Herod's rage, and when told to move again to Nazareth, fulfilling the prophecies about the Messiah.

Joseph's response to the manger reminds us that we, too, will have choices to make because Jesus has come to us. His presence in our life will not go unnoticed. There will be times when we must choose to trust and obey His word, or trust in our own wisdom and plans. Joseph could have put Mary away. God could have used another man in his place to raise the Son of God. What privilege and blessing and honor Joseph would have missed out on, had he decided to follow the dictates of his culture and disobey God, unwilling to trust – unwilling to obey!

What has God called you to do that you are struggling to trust and obey? What has He revealed to you that is His plan and purpose for your life, that seems impossible or illogical? Let's be like Joseph, and trust Him with a heart of obedient faith.

Proverbs 3:5 - *Trust in the Lord with all your heart and do not lean on your own understanding.*

PRAY TODAY
Dear Jesus, Thank You for the example of Joseph. He was just an ordinary man, with no plans for greatness. He loved a young girl and desired to marry and raise a family that honored God. But You gave Him an opportunity to do something very special, because he had a heart to trust You and obey. Help me to be fully committed to You, with a heart and mind that is devoted to obeying Your word, which gives me direction in life. As I meditate on what the manger means to me, let it remind me to trust and obey the One who came. Amen.

Day Thirteen

Take It In

And when eight days had passed, before His circumcision, His name was then called Jesus, the name given by the angel before He was conceived in the womb. And when the days for their purification according to the law of Moses were completed, they brought Him [Jesus] up to Jerusalem to present Him to the Lord (as it is written in the Law of the Lord, "Every firstborn male that opens the womb shall be called holy to the Lord"), and to offer a sacrifice according to what was said in the Law of the Lord, "A pair of turtledoves or two young pigeons." (Luke 2:22-24)

Think It Through

Here we see the faithfulness of Mary and Joseph. Knowing that their child was extraordinary...special...they might think He was exempt from the Jewish laws. After all, He was made of God Himself; *He was God.* But instead, they took special care to follow exactly every precept and ordinance God had set down for Jewish families.

The baby was circumcised on the eighth day, just as God commanded. He was named according to the angel's instructions: *Jesus.* And forty days after His birth, they made a journey to Jerusalem.

The first-born son was to be dedicated to the Lord as a reminder of God's rescue of the nation at that first Passover (Exodus 13). The parents were to make an offering, a sacrifice of the heart based on their personal financial abilities. The offerings were according to the law, to make atonement. The law required a lamb for a burnt offering and a pigeon or turtledove for a sin offering.

Luke indicates Mary and Joseph brought two pigeons or turtledoves, not a lamb. This tells us something about them: they were poor. The law contained an exemption, a provision, for those whose means were not sufficient to bring the required lamb; they could bring another pigeon instead.

Live It Out

Mary and Joseph's faithful obedience show us the importance of doing things God's way, even when we think there might be extraordinary circumstances that would give us reason to follow our own plan. And the evidence of their humble state in life reminds us that there is only one way to come to the manger...in spiritual poverty.

Jesus came to call the needy, the poor in spirit, who recognize they are spiritually bankrupt and need a Savior. We cannot seize upon the offer of salvation the manger offers with a wrong estimation of our personal worth. We must recognize that we are lost without Him, with no illusion that we are perhaps good enough to merit His favor. And we must come to God through the manger...through Jesus...for that is what He has declared to be the only way to salvation.

Matthew 5:3 – *Blessed are the poor in spirit, for theirs is the kingdom of heaven.*

PRAY TODAY

Dear Jesus, I recognize my own spiritual poverty. I do not possess any currency or achievement valuable enough to purchase my way into heaven. It is only through the sacrifice that You have required that I can come into Your presence – and that sacrifice is You. Thank You for the lessons that Mary and Joseph teach us, to follow Your plan, beginning with how we come to You in salvation and all throughout a life that is obedient to You. Thank You for the manger, that tells us that we are unworthy in ourselves, but of great value to You. Amen.

The Passion of the Manger
Day 14 – Day 18

Now when they heard this, they were pierced to the heart,
and said to Peter and the rest of the apostles,
"Brethren, what shall we do?"
Acts 2:37

By its presence in our lives, the manger evokes a response, a passion.
Some of us will embrace the Child and all He represents,
taking Him into our lives.
Others will thrust Him from our sight, and turn away from the manger.

Just like the shepherds, the wise men, Simeon,
or Herod, who tried to kill Him,
every person who comes face to face with the manger will
respond with a passion.

We cannot meet Jesus and ever be the same.

Day Fourteen

Take It In

In the same region there were some shepherds staying out in the fields and keeping watch over their flock by night. And an angel of the Lord suddenly stood before them, and the glory of the Lord shone around them; and they were terribly frightened. But the angel said to them, "Do not be afraid; for behold, I bring you good news of great joy which will be for all the people; for today in the city of David there has been born for you a Savior, who is Christ the Lord. This will be a sign for you: you will find a baby wrapped in cloths and lying in a manger." And suddenly there appeared with the angel a multitude of the heavenly host praising God and saying, "Glory to God in the highest, and on earth peace among men with whom He is pleased." (Luke 2:8-14)

Think It Through

Close your eyes. Imagine you are a humble shepherd sitting out in a field with your fellow shepherds, chatting quietly in the dark. It's an unseasonably warm night, and the sheep are bunched closely together, resting. You have no reason to expect that this night is any different than the hundreds you've spent just like it. Suddenly, out of nowhere, a man appears in front of you. Dressed in brilliant white, light surrounds him and envelops you and your friends. Immediately you realize that this is no ordinary man, and that you have a heavenly visitor. In the brightness of the light, your heart pounds and you experience fear, shock and amazement. You are speechless.

The angel's voice rings out with authority, with an unbelievable message: a Savior has been born! While you are processing this news, he goes on to give details about the baby. Just when you are coming to terms with the presence of one angel, thousands more fill the sky, lighting it up as though it were noon instead of the middle of the night, all loudly proclaiming glory to God. At the end of their song, they disappear – light swallowed up in darkness, and the earth is quiet as if nothing had happened.

Can you imagine what the shepherds thought as they looked at one another? I'm sure at first, they were confused, all talking at once. Then one suggests, "Let's go find this baby." There may have been some discussion, some thought, but the end result was that a group of rough shepherds made their way to Bethlehem to see if the angel had been telling the truth. They went to investigate the manger.

Live It Out

The shepherds experienced physically what each one of us face spiritually. They were in darkness, under the cover of night, when the light of the glory of the Lord suddenly shone on them. For a few short minutes, as the angel delivered his message and then was joined by the multitude praising God, everything was clearly seen. The darkness had been pushed back by the light. And as suddenly as they had come, they were gone, and the shepherds were again clothed in darkness.

In the same way, we are all given glimpses of the glory of God. Unexpectedly, while going about our normal business of life, God opens our eyes to the truth. For a moment, we see. We understand our own need of God and feel the conviction of our sin. The curtain of spiritual darkness is drawn back and we get to peek inside at the love and grace and mercy of God that calls to us. Then the curtain falls, and we are again in darkness, left to decide what our response will be.

Isaiah 9:2, describing both the physical and the spiritual, says it this way: *The people who walk in darkness will see a great light; those who live in a dark land, the light will shine on them.* Have you seen the great light? Has God opened your eyes, even briefly, to the truth of salvation – to the good news that a Savior has come? The shepherds decided to take the angel's word and go and find the manger. Have you?

2 Corinthians 4:6 - *For God, who said, "Light shall shine out of darkness," is the One who has shone in our hearts to give the Light of the knowledge of the glory of God in the face of Christ.*

PRAY TODAY
Dear Jesus, I thank You for shining the light of truth into my life. Without You, I would continue to walk in darkness, unaware of my own sin and my separation from You. I could not find You on my own, but You loved me and called out to me. Just like the shepherds, I must respond to the light that pushes back the darkness. I must believe, and come to You. Thank You for calling me and showing me the truth. Amen.

Day Fifteen

Take It In
When the angels had gone away from them into heaven, the shepherds began saying to one another, "Let us go straight to Bethlehem then, and see this thing that has happened which the Lord has made known to us." So they came in a hurry and found their way to Mary and Joseph, and the baby as He lay in the manger. When they had seen this, they made known the statement which had been told them about this Child. And all who heard it wondered at the things

which were told them by the shepherds. ... The shepherds went back, glorifying and praising God for all that they had heard and seen, just as had been told them. (Luke 2:15-18, 20)

Think It Through

Why do you think God chose shepherds to receive the news about the birth of the Savior? We could speculate, but I believe it was because God knew what their response would be. He chose them because He could trust them with the news.

The shepherds recognized that the Lord (Creator God) had revealed something terribly precious and exciting. He had *made it known* to them. Their immediate response (quickly, hurriedly), was to go straight to Bethlehem to see. It doesn't appear that they doubted for a minute they would find a baby. They believed, and acted. The Greek word "made known" is to communicate, to come to know, to discover, to understand. It means more than just to "tell" ... the word implies that the listener has received the message, and understood it.

Have you ever checked the box "I accept" on a website, referring to terms of an agreement, without reading them? Of course you have (we've all done it)! Or signed at the doctor's office that you received a copy of some form, but failed to read it? That's the difference in just *telling* someone, and *making it known*! We are told many things in our life, but it is the information we accept and believe that becomes true *knowledge* – something made known to us.

When the shepherds heard the message of the manger, God *made it known* to them. They didn't just hear the words, but the words had an impact on their heart and mind. Something stirred within them that told them "this is true...listen!" So they acted on what had been made known.

Live It Out

What did the shepherds find, when they responded to what God had made known? They discovered He had told them the truth! The baby was there – right in the manger, where the angel had said He would be. As they excitedly shared with Mary and Joseph their experience, I'm sure the proud parents filled them in on the miracle of the baby's conception. And this knowledge didn't stay with the shepherds, but caused them to passionately respond: they went out and *made known* all these things. They left the manger praising and glorifying God, speaking about what they had seen.

What has God made known to you? When we look at the manger, we realize that God has been speaking the truth to our heart and mind. The Savior has come, and we have heard the good news. Will we believe and act on what we know? And to whom will we make it known?

Psalm 98:2 - *The Lord has made known His salvation; He has revealed His righteousness in the sight of the nations.*

PRAY TODAY
Dear Jesus, Many times I have heard Your voice – through preachers, friends, teachers, family, and especially through Your word. You are Truth, and You desire to make Yourself known to me. Help me to believe and act on what You make known to me. Keep me from doubts and my own beliefs that would prevent me from seeing who You really are. I want to respond like the shepherds – believing and acting on the wonderful news that Your manger represents. Amen.

Day Sixteen

Take It In
And there was a man in Jerusalem whose name was Simeon; and this man was righteous and devout, looking for the consolation of Israel; and the Holy Spirit was upon him. And it had been revealed to him by the Holy Spirit that he would not see death before he had seen the Lord's Christ. (Luke 2:25-26)

Think It Through
Meet Simeon. We picture him as an old man, but we don't know his actual age. He is described as righteous and devout, a worshipper, with the Holy Spirit of God upon him. We find him in the temple. We learn here that he had a life-long purpose, to see Israel restored to the great and blessed nation promised by the prophets: he was looking for the *consolation of Israel.*

"Consolation" means comfort, solace, refreshment. It is a variation of the same Greek root word that describes the Holy Spirit as "Comforter" in John 14:16. The Jews of Simeon's day were living under Roman occupation; they were free to worship their God as long as they paid their taxes and obeyed Roman law. They were surrounded by pagan gods and practices, and treated at best as second-class citizens, and often as slaves. Life was hard, and they longed for true freedom, to be the people of God they knew was God's original intention for the nation. They were waiting for God to bring the refreshment and solace of His kingdom restored, as He had foretold.

According to the rest of the passage in Luke 2 (see verses 27-35), when Simeon held the infant Jesus in his arms, he declared that he was ready to die. He had spent his whole life looking for the redemption and restoration of Israel, and he found it when he looked into the sleepy eyes of a *baby*? His words of praise tell us that he knew this was no ordinary child: *For my eyes have seen Your salvation, which You have prepared in the presence of all peoples, a light of revelation to the Gentiles, and the glory of Your people Israel.*

Live It Out

Simeon's passionate response to Jesus vividly illustrates the response of mankind looking for comfort and restoration. We are broken people, separated from our Creator, and living in a world that is dominated by our enemy – Satan. We are surrounded by false gods and beliefs. Before we even meet Jesus, there is a desire in our hearts for something we cannot find in this life. In our soul, we crave satisfaction and fulfillment; we long to feel complete...to be comforted and refreshed.

That yearning is the desire of the one created to be comforted by their Creator. It is Jesus, the baby in the manger, who will be our consolation. What must we do to gain this consolation, this fulfillment of our soul? We must do just as Simeon did. As he received the baby from his mother's arms, so we receive Jesus into our lives. We look on Him, and we believe, and our eyes will see salvation.

Isaiah 52:9-10 - *Break forth, shout joyfully together, you waste places of Jerusalem; for the Lord has comforted His people, He has redeemed Jerusalem. The Lord has bared His holy arm in the sight of all the nations, that all the ends of the earth may see the salvation of our God.*

PRAY TODAY
*Dear Jesus, We would love to have been present when Simeon first held You in his arms and Your Holy Spirit whispered to his soul that **this** was who he had been waiting for. What joy must have lit up his face! We experience that same joy when we understand and see You for who You are – our consolation and salvation. Thank You for being the One who satisfies our longing to be restored. Amen.*

Take It In

Now after Jesus was born in Bethlehem of Judea in the days of Herod the king, magi from the east arrived in Jerusalem, saying, "Where is He who has been born King of the Jews? For we saw His star in the east and have come to worship Him." ... After hearing the king, they went their way; and the star, which they had seen in the east, went on before them until it came and stood over the place where the Child was. When they saw the star, they rejoiced exceedingly with great joy. After coming into the house they saw the Child with Mary His mother and they fell to the ground and worshiped Him. Then, opening their treasures, they presented to Him gifts of gold, frankincense and myrrh. (Matthew 2:1-2,9-11)

Think It Through

The role of the magi is a coveted one in every children's Christmas program. After all, you get to wear a crown and a fancy robe, and if you're part of extravagant displays, there might even be camels! We associate the magi's visit with Jesus' birth, though most likely the baby had become a lively two-year-old by the time they arrived in Bethlehem.

The magi, or wise men, were a caste of men who specialized in astronomy, astrology and natural sciences. They were highly intelligent, curious, and learned. They spent their lives studying the physical world but they also knew history. They would have been familiar with prophecy from many cultures, and God had allowed them to understand that a star would appear to announce a new king of Israel. Scholars believe they may have referred to Balaam's prophecy in Numbers 24:17 which reads *"I see him, but not now; I behold him, but not near; a star shall come forth from Jacob, a scepter shall rise from Israel"* and understood it in conjunction with Daniel's prophecies that foretold the time of the Messiah's arrival. So, they were looking for, and anticipating this star, and when it appeared, they knew what it meant.

We often think there were only three magi, because there were three gifts. More likely this was quite an entourage, consisting of more than a dozen wise men, along with their horses, servants and traveling companions. These were rich and powerful men, and they would not have made the long journey alone. No wonder Herod took notice when they arrived in his court!

When the magi finally saw the "king" they sought, what was their response? They didn't question His humble beginnings or His circumstances. They recognized Him immediately as the fulfillment of the prophecies. They believed the star had led them to the right place, at the right time, to the right

Person. They fell down and worshipped – even laying prostrate before this little boy. This must have been an amazing experience for Mary and Joseph!

Live It Out

Just like God gave the magi the wisdom and understanding to look for the star and follow it, He gives us signs every day that He has come, and that He is the King. Some of these signs are biblical – the fulfillment of prophecies made thousands of years ago. But some are more tangible to us. The beauty of the sunrise, faithfully greeting us *every single morning.* The change of the seasons, showing us the cycle of life, death, and new life again. The doors He opens, the people He brings into our life, the provision of our needs. Each blessing, each trial, each change is sign that God is actively pursuing us, calling us to notice that He has come to be our King.

The magi were looking for the King. They anticipated the sign of the star, so they recognized it. What is refreshing is that their intelligence and understanding of the physical world did not cause them to doubt, but led them straight to the worship of their Creator. How has God been speaking to you, and have you recognized that it is Him? And will you respond with the same passion of the magi, and worship the King?

Psalm 95:6 - *Come, let us worship and bow down, let us kneel before the Lord our Maker.*

PRAY TODAY
Dear Jesus, Thank You for the many, many ways You speak to us, drawing us to Yourself before we even recognize that it is You! Forgive us when we overlook the signs of Your presence, Your care, and Your love for us. Help us to respond as the magi did – in simple worship, surrendering ourselves and our treasures to You. Amen.

Day Eighteen

Take It In

Then Herod secretly called the magi and determined from them the exact time the star appeared. And he sent them to Bethlehem and said, "Go and search carefully for the Child; and when you have found Him, report to me, so that I too may come and worship Him." ... Then when Herod saw that he had been tricked by the magi, he became very enraged, and sent and slew all the male children who were in Bethlehem and all its vicinity, from two years old and under, according to the time which he had determined from the magi. (Matthew 2:7-8, 16)

Think It Through

Herod's part in the story of Jesus' birth and early years is not one we like to remember. It's an ugly story. Herod the Great was appointed by the Roman government to rule over the Jewish state. He's been referred to as "brutal, self-delusional, and murderous." His position was secure only if he kept the Jews under control, enforcing Roman law and taxes, and causing no attention that would draw Caesar's wrath.

Herod's actions after he was made aware of the birth of Jesus are telling. He believed the magi's story, and consulted with the religious leaders of the Jews to find out where the baby would have been born. He obviously saw the baby as a threat to the fragile balance of power he held as a puppet king, and set out to destroy his perceived competition. Herod lied straightforward to the magi, pretending that he wanted to also worship the Child. He asked them to report back as soon as they found Him. God had a different plan, however, and sent the magi away. Realizing he had been tricked sent Herod into a rage. Determined to protect his own throne, he sent his soldiers to kill every child under two years of age in Bethlehem and the surrounding villages.

I cannot imagine the horror of having a Roman soldier tear your baby from your arms to kill him in front of you. What motivated Herod's actions? How could a man be so cruel, so angry, so vile? Was there not a shred of humanity in his soul? Did he have no conscience?

Live It Out

Herod's passionate response to the manger reveals what was in his heart, and who he really served (John 8:44). Fearful for his own position and power, he did what he felt was necessary to defend himself, regardless of the pain and devastation it caused. He was "god" in his own eyes, and his actions reveal this.

Are we ever like Herod? We would not conceive of killing innocent children to protect ourselves. But do we ever pretend to be worshippers of Jesus to get something we want? Do we accept as truth that Jesus was born to be King, but do everything in our power to keep Him away from the throne of our heart?

The manger stirs in each of us a passion. We are either awakened to worship, or incited to reject. Our response will reveal who is on the throne of our heart.

John 10:10 - *The thief comes only to steal and kill and destroy; I came that they may have life, and have it abundantly.*

PRAY TODAY

Dear Jesus, Herod's story makes us all stop and think about who we really are in our heart of hearts. Without You, our human flesh will do everything possible to protect our own interests – even unspeakable, horrible things. It is only in surrendering to You and allowing You to be in Your rightful place on the throne of our heart that we find peace. Help us not to be deceived by our enemy, who desires to destroy us, and leads us away from You. Amen.

The Power of the Manger
Day 19 – Day 24

*For the word of the cross is foolishness to those who are perishing, but to us
who are being saved it is the power of God. ... But we preach
Christ crucified, to Jews a stumbling block and to Gentiles foolishness,
but to those who are the called, both Jews and Greeks,
Christ the power of God and the wisdom of God.*
1 Corinthians 1:18,23-24

The power of the manger is life change. It's simple cause and effect.

God's redemption plan is the cause.
God sent His Son into our world as a human baby to live a perfect, sinless
life, be crucified on a Roman cross for the sins of the world, and raise to
new life, defeating death. These are powerful, life-changing truths.

Our new life is the effect.
We begin as spiritual babies and grow up. We learn to worship God for
who He really is. He speaks to us through His Word, and
we respond in prayer. And we no longer walk in sinful ways,
but learn to live holy lives pleasing to our Father.
Things are different now.

Day Nineteen

Take It In

Jesus answered and said to him, "Truly, truly, I say to you, unless one is born again he cannot see the kingdom of God." Nicodemus said to Him, "How can a man be born when he is old? He cannot enter a second time into his mother's womb and be born, can he?" Jesus answered, "Truly, truly, I say to you, unless one is born of water and the Spirit, he cannot enter into the kingdom of God." (John 3:3-5)

Think It Through

New life. That is the miracle of birth. Before a child is conceived, there is no life in the womb. It is empty, dead. The womb cannot create a life on its own – the seed of life must be implanted. We are very familiar with how new life comes about physically; the pro-creation of humans and animals is as old as creation itself. Jesus came by way of birth to show us the way to *new life.*

My husband and I recently experienced the arrival of our first grandchild. I was in the room when she transitioned from her mother's womb into the world. After all the toil of labor, the sound we waited anxiously to hear was those first cries - indisputable evidence that *new life had arrived!*

The manger reminds us that while Mary and Joseph rejoiced to hear the cries of Jesus as He was born, His entrance into the world declared more than His own physical life had begun; new life for all mankind would now be possible.

Live It Out

When a baby is born, his life dramatically changes. His environment, the way he breathes, how he takes in nourishment; everything is different. There are new sounds, new sights. His life is instantly (and abruptly) altered. And just as Nicodemus so clearly stated, he cannot return to his mother's womb. The fact of his birth is established. No one can argue that a baby has arrived, and he cannot return to his "old" life. It's simply not possible.

Jesus' arrival as a baby illustrates what happens when a person accepts the good news of salvation and is born into the kingdom of God. New life has begun. We have a new beginning, and a new history to write. Scripture tells us that the old things (our old life) has passed away, and that all things have become new (2 Corinthians 5:17), and that our new life is lived out by the indwelling Spirit of Christ in us (Galatians 2:20).

Your life after being born into the kingdom of God will change dramatically. There will be evidence that something has happened. The manger speaks of the power of life, and its impact on us is significant. From death to life, from old to new, we are born again.

Romans 6:4 – *Therefore we have been buried with Him through baptism into death, so that as Christ was raised from the dead through the glory of the Father, so we too might walk in newness of life.*

PRAY TODAY
Dear Jesus, A physical birth is a glorious and amazing thing, but it's also a painful event! There are long hours of toil and labor to go through before the joy of a new life is experienced. That is often true of our spiritual birth. We are stubborn and willful, and in the process of coming to You we must be willing to give up our old life and enter into the new way of life You offer. Thank You for being patient with us, for enduring with us, until we are born again. Teach us how to live this new life You have given us. Amen.

Day Twenty

Take It In
The Child continued to grow and become strong, increasing in wisdom; and the grace of God was upon Him. ... And Jesus kept increasing in wisdom and stature, and in favor with God and men. (Luke 2:40,52)

Think It Through
The Bible reveals little about the boy Jesus – this baby who started life in a manger. We have record of only one event when He was twelve years old; He stayed behind in Jerusalem when His parents assumed He was with the family caravan. Much later (three days, in fact), they finally discovered Him sitting in the temple having theological discussions with the rabbis.

What was this little boy like? These two verses in Luke give us an idea. First, He grew, just as any other child. Not just physically (stature) but spiritually. The original language in verse 40 says He *became strong in spirit.* As His physical mind and body developed, He grew in spiritual understanding, of who He was, and why He had been born.

Second, He increased in wisdom. When the Son of God was born, He *emptied Himself...made in the likeness of men* (Philippians 2:7). The phrase literally means He *laid aside His privileges.* Existing as God, He had all wisdom and as the One who cannot change, He had no need to increase in anything. But for our example, He became a child who had to learn to apply the knowledge He gained each day – He grew wise.

Third, the grace of God was upon Him, and as He grew, this grace spilled over into the lives of others. Grace is the favor, delight, and pleasure of God. It speaks of joy. Jesus was a delightful child, a pleasure to be with, and as He grew to manhood, His words, actions, thoughts, and deeds exemplified the grace of God that was on His life.

Live It Out

Jesus' physical life models our spiritual life. We are born into the kingdom of God, and are spiritual babies at the time of our new birth. But just as Jesus grew, we are to grow in our faith and walk as a Christ-follower. 1 Peter 2:2 tells us *like newborn babies, long for the pure milk of the word, so that by it you may **grow** in respect to salvation.*

Spiritual growth is a gift from our loving Father. Often, a person will have doubts and fears about accepting God's invitation to salvation, because they feel unworthy, or unable to "meet God's expectations" or that they could be a "good Christian." But just as Jesus' mother, Mary, would have delighted in watching her Son grow into a man full of the grace of God, so our Heavenly Father patiently and lovingly grows us up spiritually into Christ-likeness. In fact, He delights in seeing us become established in our faith, and equipped to carry out the work He has planned for us.

The manger reminds us that we all come to faith as newborn babies, but that we do not remain spiritually immature. Just as Jesus grew, we become men and women of strong spiritual faith, applying the wisdom and knowledge of the Word, and living in the grace of God so that it spills over to those around us.

Colossians 2:6-7 – *Therefore as you have received Christ Jesus the Lord, so walk in Him, having been firmly rooted and now being built up in Him and established in your faith, just as you were instructed, and overflowing with gratitude.*

PRAY TODAY
Dear Jesus, Thank You for not leaving us as spiritual babies. When You welcome us into Your family, You immediately begin teaching us and growing us into Your likeness. Your life here as a child who had to grow up reminds us of our responsibility to become mature men and women of faith. The manger welcomed You, but it did not hold You forever. Help us to become the spiritual adults You desire us to be. Amen.

Take It In

After hearing the king, they [the magi] went their way; and the star, which they had seen in the east, went on before them until it came and stood over the place where the Child was. When they saw the star, they rejoiced exceedingly with great joy. After coming into the house they saw the Child with Mary His mother, and they fell to the ground and worshiped Him. Then, opening their treasures, they presented to Him gifts of gold, frankincense, and myrrh. (Matthew 2:9-11)

Think It Through

When the wise men came calling, Mary and Joseph had not yet returned to Nazareth, but were living in a house in Bethlehem. Almost three years had passed since the angel first visited Mary. I imagine they had settled into a routine, like every other couple whose lives have been turned upside down by the arrival of a newborn. While they could not forget the origin of Jesus' birth, the days now had a simpler rhythm, with Mary caring for the toddler, and Joseph working as a carpenter to support them. Suddenly, into their small world, came an entourage of wealthy men, climbing down off their animals and filling their small house with strange sights and smells. They were abruptly brought back to the extraordinary reality of Jesus' true parentage – Holy God.

What can we learn from the magi's worship of the Child of the manger?

Their worship was full of joy and delight, as they realized the star had brought them to their destination. Their worship was expressed in humility, as royalty bowed before a little child. And their worship was offered in generosity, as they opened their treasures and gave gifts.

To our cultural mindset, these were strange gifts for a baby. Whether the magi realized it or not, their gifts told the story of why Jesus came, and who He really was. Gold speaks of His **deity**, His royalty. Jesus is our King, the Son of God come down from heaven. Frankincense speaks of **sacrifice**. Jesus is our High Priest, who offered Himself as the sin offering. Myrrh speaks of **death**, the spice used in embalming. Jesus laid His own life, experiencing death in our place.

Live It Out

The gifts of the magi teach us something about how we are to worship God. It has been said that idolatry is any thought of God that is less than He is. In other words, we must worship God for who He is, not who we think Him to

47

be. We cannot love Him until we worship Him as Lord and King of our lives, recognizing Him as the sacrifice for our sin, and believing in His death and resurrection.

The gifts also speak of our worship after salvation, as we offer ourselves back to Him. We are tried as gold, to become pure vessels (Job 23:10). We are to become living sacrifices, not conformed to this world, but transformed (Romans 12:1-2). And we are to die to ourselves by daily taking up our cross, denying self, and following Him (Mark 8:34).

Tried as gold. Living sacrifices. Dying to self. These are the gifts we offer the Child of the manger. Will we be wise men, too, who come with joy and humility, opening our hearts and lives to worship the King?

Psalm 132:7 - *Let us go into His dwelling place; Let us worship at His footstool.*

PRAY TODAY
Dear Jesus, I'm not sure the wise men realized the prophetic implications of the gifts they laid at Your feet. But that's so often the case with our worship – we lift our hands, our voices, and our lives to You, but do we truly understand who You are, and what we are saying as we proclaim our love for You and offer You our lives? Thank You for accepting the worship of imperfect people. Thank You for making a way into Your presence. Teach us how to worship You humbly, joyfully and with generosity. Amen.

Day Twenty-Two

Take It In
God, after He spoke long ago to the fathers in the prophets in many portions and in many ways, in these last days has spoken to us in His Son, whom He appointed heir of all things, through whom also He made the world. And He is the radiance of His glory and the exact representation of His nature, and upholds all things by the word of His power. (Hebrews 1:1-3a)

Think It Through
Has God ever spoken to you? I always find it interesting when people tell me, "God told me..." Personally, I have never heard the voice of God speak to me out loud, though there have been many times I wished that He would! It would make it so much easier to believe in Him, to trust Him. Or would it?

God speaks to us every day, through His creation. According to Romans 1:20, creation displays His invisible attributes, His eternal power and His divine nature so clearly that *all men are without excuse.* In other words, none of us can claim ignorance about God. We cannot deny Him. God has also spoken through His Old Testament prophets – the Word which has been written down for us – thousands of years of testimony pointing to the manger, where God would speak most loudly and clearly in these last days, in His Son. We might say Jesus is God's "final word," His most important revelation.

Jesus is the radiance of God's glory, and the exact representation of God's nature. Jesus is God saying, "this is Me." God desired to communicate with us, to show us who He is and what He is like, so Jesus came, the very brightness of the glory of God. When we see Jesus, we see God. When we hear Jesus' words, we hear God. When we love Jesus, we love God. And if we reject Jesus, we reject God.

Live It Out

When someone speaks to you, they expect you to answer. That is why we call it "communication." It is a *conversation.* God did not send His Son, Jesus, to simply make a statement. He invites us to converse with Him – to communicate. How do we do this? We respond to Jesus, the Living Word of God. It begins with a prayer of salvation, a reply of "yes." The conversation continues for the rest of our lives, as we pray to God and He speaks to us in His Word.

The manger tells us that God wants to talk. Our conversation begins when we recognize Jesus for who He is, see the glory of God and respond.

2 Corinthians 4:3-6 – *And even if our gospel is veiled, it is veiled to those who are perishing, in whose case the god of this world has blinded the minds of the unbelieving so that they might not see the light of the gospel of the glory of Christ, who is the image of God. ... For God, who said, "Light shall shine out of darkness," is the One who has shone in our hearts to give the Light of the knowledge of the glory of God, in the face of Christ.*

PRAY TODAY
Dear Jesus, Thank You for coming to reveal who God is, and what He is like. The Father loves us, and You came, not just to tell us, but to show us by how You lived and died, and rose again. You are God, speaking to us. Help us to respond. Open our eyes to see the glory of God that shines in our darkness. And as followers of You, let the manger remind us that You long to hear our prayers as we speak to You. Thank You for inviting us into this conversation with the One True God. Amen.

Take It In

Now when they had gone, behold, an angel of the Lord appeared to Joseph in a dream and said, "Get up! Take the Child and His mother and flee to Egypt, and remain there until I tell you, for Herod is going to search for the Child to destroy Him." So Joseph got up and took the Child and His mother while it was still night and left for Egypt. (Matthew 2:13-14)

Think It Through

This event in young Jesus' life illustrates two great truths: God protects His own, and He tells us what we need to know. When Joseph and Mary went to bed that night, they had just experienced a great outpouring of love and care. The Child had been worshipped by the wise men, and showered with valuable treasures. As a parent, they were probably wondering if their life had taken a turn for the better, that the Child would bring notoriety and fame and fortune. Joseph went to bed thinking the world loved His child, and was awakened by the Lord's angel telling him the king wanted to kill Him!

Joseph was faced with a choice. He could depend on his own understanding of the situation, and based on the wise men's actions, stay in Bethlehem, believing his family was safe. Or, he could take God at His word, and leave immediately. Joseph believed God, and obeyed. While it was still night, they packed up their belongings and fled to Egypt.

As a young child himself, Joseph would have learned the Psalms at his own mother's feet. Perhaps Psalm 91:11 came to mind when he awoke from his dream: *For He will give His angels charge concerning you, to guard you in all your ways.* Or Psalm 121:8, which reminded him *The Lord will guard your going out and your coming in.* Because Joseph knew the promises of God in His word, he had no hesitation in trusting what God said to him.

Live It Out

God still protects His children, and He still tells us what we need to know. While He spoke to Joseph through an angel in a dream, Joseph relied on what He knew of God in His word to assure him the message was true. God's word confirmed the character of God, and gave confidence that what the angel said could be trusted.

God has given us the written Word to direct our steps and protect our path. His instructions and commands guard our lives, giving us boundaries and guidance. It is the foundation of our walk in Christ, and it is only in reading, studying, believing and obeying God's Word that we can develop a confident and sure faith.

The manger reminds us of the power of God's Word. Do you believe it, or will you trust in yourself? Like Joseph, we have a choice, to rely on our own logic and understanding, or take God at His Word, and live.

Psalm 18:30 - *As for God, His way is blameless; the word of the Lord is tried; He is a shield to all who take refuge in Him.*

PRAY TODAY
Dear Jesus, Thank You for always telling us what we need to know. You have given us Your written Word so that we have direction for every step of life, and answers to all our questions. You have not left us to stumble about in darkness, but have made Your word the light for our path. Help us to be like Joseph, to trust Your Word immediately and obey. Amen.

Day Twenty-Four

Take It In
She will bear a Son; and you shall call His name Jesus, for He will save His people from their sins. (Matthew 1:21)

You know that He appeared in order to take away sins; and in Him there is no sin. (Hebrews 3:5)

Think It Through
There's nothing sweeter than a newborn baby. A baby is the promise of new life, a fresh start, a new beginning. They have no history of failures; no sinful past. They speak of purity and innocence, and of all good things. Sadly, because of our fallen nature, it doesn't take long for a young life to be filled with regrets. Sin destroys, and its favorite thing to devastate is a human life.

We cannot think of the innocent baby in the manger without thinking of sin, for sin is why Jesus came. His very existence defied sin, being born of a virgin, conceived by the Holy Spirit, and escaping the sinful nature of men by having no earthly father. He was born perfect, and lived a faultless life without sin (1 Peter 2:22), so that he could be the pure and sinless sacrifice – the payment for our sins.

2 Corinthians 5:21 says it this way: *He made Him who knew no sin to be sin on our behalf, so that we might become the righteousness of God in Him.* Mary's innocent baby would grow to be a righteous and holy man, bearing the weight of the sins of the world on the cross. He took our sinfulness, so that we could be made sinless.

Live It Out

How would you feel if you committed a horrible crime, and were sentenced to death? What would it mean to you if someone loved you enough to sit in your place in the electric chair, so that you could go free? This is exactly what Jesus did – He took the punishment of God's wrath against sin in our place.

The power of the manger is freedom from sin. Jesus frees us from our sinful condition and reconciles us to God. But He also frees us from sin's rule in our daily life. Because He overcame sin and death, in Him we are liberated from sin's grasp on our heart and mind. This is our life as a believer – to learn to walk in holiness, just as Christ is holy (1 Peter 1:16).

As the manger was filled with the purity and innocence of a new life, so Christ offers us new life in salvation. We no longer live for ourselves, but for Him. Have you accepted this gift of new life? And are you walking in holiness and victory over sin, in gratitude for what He did for you? In Christ, we are holy. Let's live like it.

2 Corinthians 5:15,17 – *And He died for all, so that they who live might no longer live for themselves, but for Him who died and rose again on their behalf. ... Therefore if anyone is in Christ, he is a new creature; the old things passed away; behold, new things have come.*

PRAY TODAY
Dear Jesus, Thank You for taking our sins away. Thank You for the promise of new life that we see in a sweet and innocent baby. You came into this world to show us what holiness looks like. And because You loved us, You made a way for us to be holy in You. Help us to live holy lives. We owe You everything, and desire to be pleasing to You. Amen.

The People of the Manger
Day 25 – Day 31

But you are a chosen race, a royal priesthood, a holy nation,
a people for God's own possession, so that you may proclaim the excellencies
of Him who has called you out of darkness into His marvelous light;
for you once were not a people, but now you are the people of God; you had
not received mercy, but now you have received mercy.
1 Peter 2:9-10

When we are born into the kingdom of God, by the power
of the manger, we are not left alone. We become part of
a unique and living body known as the church. We become part of
a family of believers. We encourage one another,
worship together, serve in partnership, and use our strengths and
weaknesses to bring to light the grace and mercy of God,
as we show others the way to become part of the family too.
Most of all, we reveal the glory of God.

Take It In

But Mary treasured all these things, pondering them in her heart. ...And He [Jesus] went down with them and came to Nazareth, and He continued in subjection to them; and His mother treasured all these things in her heart. (Luke 2:19,51)

But we proved to be gentle among you, as a nursing mother tenderly cares for her own children. Having so fond an affection for you, we were well-pleased to impart to you not only the gospel of God, but also our own lives, because you had become very dear to us. ... Just as you know how we were exhorting and encouraging and imploring each one of you as a father would his own children. (1 Thessalonians 2:7-8,11)

Think It Through

One of my favorite parts of decorating for Christmas is setting up the nativity scene. Somehow, placing each piece in its proper place takes me back to that first Christmas morning. Mary and Joseph are always carefully settled close to the manger, to protect and gaze on this little miracle. Their lives were forever changed.

We assume they were thinking about the unbelievable, that they would be raising the Son of God, but I believe Mary's thoughts in that moment were as any other new mother – she immediately and unconditionally loved this little Child. Mary wasn't thinking about the task ahead; she simply and naturally moved into her role as mother, to nurture, protect, encourage, and teach. She felt things deeply, treasuring these memories of raising the Child, and allowing God to lead her day by day. After all, God had chosen her, so she embraced the role gladly.

Paul's illustration of a nursing mother connects beautifully to the example of Mary's love for Jesus. Just as Mary and Joseph stepped into their roles as the physical mother and father of Jesus, so we are to be spiritual parents to new believers. We tenderly care for one another, sharing not just the words of the gospel, but our very lives. Mary's life was now focused on this baby, to provide everything He needed to grow. We do the same for one another.

Live It Out

When we are born into the family of God, we have spiritual parents (the people who tell us about Jesus), and spiritual brothers and sisters (other Christ-followers who love and care for us). And as we grow up in our faith

faith, we become family to others, by sharing the good news about Jesus, and encouraging, exhorting, teaching and loving them as brothers and sisters. We become responsible for one another.

Jesus makes us family. He gives us a love and affection for one another, and teaches how to live. Who is it that God has placed in your life to be a spiritual mother or father to? And who has reached out to you in the love of Christ, inviting you into the family?

1 John 3:1 - *See how great a love the Father has bestowed on us, that we would be called children of God; and such we are.*

PRAY TODAY
Dear Jesus, Thank You for making us family. You call us Your brothers and sisters, and Your Father is our Father. Because we are family, we care for one another, just like Mary cared for You when You were a baby. Thank You for giving us spiritual brothers and sisters. Help us to be willing to give our lives up for each other, to do whatever it takes to bring others into the family, and encourage them to grow up in Your likeness. Amen.

Day Twenty-Six

Take It In
For this reason I bow my knees before the Father, from whom every family in heaven and on earth derives its name, that He would grant you, according to the riches of His glory, to be strengthened with power through His Spirit in the inner man, so that Christ may dwell in your hearts through faith; and that you, being rooted and ground in love, may be able to comprehend with all the saints what is the breadth and length and height and depth, and to know the love of Christ which surpasses knowledge, that you may be filled up to all the fulness of Christ. (Ephesians 3:14-19)

Think It Through
Here Paul uses a play on words. He prays to the Father about the family. The word for **father**, used here in reference to God, our Heavenly Father, is *pater*, literally the generator or male ancestor-the one who begins the **family**, from the Greek word *patria*, meaning the lineage running back to some progenitor. In other words, the root word of *family*, is *father*.

A father is the author of a family or society of persons animated by the same spirit as himself; one who has infused his own spirit into others. A family is all those who in a given people lay claim to a common origin. ***The family is formed out of the father.***

When my daughter labored to bring our first grandchild into the world, she did not labor alone. She was supported by her husband, the *pater*, father, of this child, along with me, her mom and self-appointed cheerleader/coach, and a sympathetic and knowledgeable staff of nurses, doctor, technicians, and anesthesiologist. We labored alongside, and were present when this tiny baby took her first breaths and filled the room with the sound of those beautiful newborn baby cries.

But we weren't the only ones participating in this entrance into life. In a special room down the hall, another group of people labored too, in prayer, encouragement and support. This little one was born into the *family* created by the *Father*, specifically for her. Her appearance, after many long hours, instantly made us all grandmothers and grandfathers, aunts and uncles. The family grew in number, but also in heart. What we experienced and shared makes us *family*.

Live It Out

This concept of family became tangible to me in a whole new way, along with a greater understanding of what really took place at the manger. Just as Jesus' newborn cries made a family out of Mary and Joseph, our spiritual family grows when a person becomes a believer, and is born into the family of God. The process of new birth is messy, difficult, and long. It is humbling, and dependent on others. At times, it seems the new life will never arrive. It is painful. It is hard labor to see a baby born into the family.

So, too, someone labored to bring us into the kingdom. New (spiritual) birth is experienced when the whole family is involved. Someone waits and prays for us. Others show us the way by example and experience. Others cheer us on, encouraging us. Someone labors in reasoning with us. Still, others take hold of us and boldly, confidently, bring us into life; they lead us to the manger, where we meet the One who makes us family, our progenitor, our *pater*, our Father.

The manger reminds us of family, and the life Christ came to give. Have you been born again into the kingdom? If so, stop and thank God for those who labored to bring you into this new life, and think about the role you are to play in helping others experience this same new life. And if you are not yet part of God's family, know that there are family members who are anxiously awaiting your arrival, who are laboring for you to be born and meet your Father.

1 Timothy 1:1-2 – *Paul, an apostle of Christ Jesus according to the commandment of God our Savior, and of Christ Jesus, who is our hope. To Timothy, my true child in the faith: Grace, mercy and peace from God the Father and Christ Jesus our Lord.*

PRAY TODAY
Dear Jesus, In You, we are made family. Out of the Father's love, through Your Spirit and because of Your willingness to be born into our world, we have the opportunity to become part of Your family, along with all those who believe. Thank You for those who labored for me to be born again. Help me to understand the miracle of new life in You, and become someone who labors for others to come into Your family. Amen.

Day Twenty-Seven

Take It In
For He Himself is our peace, who made both groups into one and broke down the barrier of the dividing wall, by abolishing in His flesh the enmity, which is the Law of commandments contained in the ordinances, so that in Himself He might make the two into one new man, thus establishing peace, and might reconcile them both in one body to God through the cross, by it having put to death the enmity. (Ephesians 2:14-16)

Therefore, since the children share in flesh and blood, He Himself likewise also partook of the same, that through death He might render powerless him who had the power of death, that is, the devil, and might free those who through fear of death were subject to slavery all their lives. (Hebrews 2:14-15)

Think It Through
The Christian faith is built on many foundational truths, but one stands out as the most unbelievable, the biggest hurdle to salvation. The religious Jews, the most learned men of Old Testament scripture, stumbled over this truth: God was born in a human body. How could the Creator of the Universe, One who is Spirit, transcendent above our world, be contained in a tiny baby's body? And why would He choose to do this?

The manger, cradling human flesh, reminds us that God came to us in a mortal body, and He came this way for specific reasons, to accomplish certain pre-ordained purposes, and to teach us valuable lessons about who we are and how we live as Christ-followers.

Jesus came in a body to share in our human flesh, in order to die. He had to be made like us in order to redeem us. The result of sin is death, and death had to be conquered. Only God could do this, and He did it by going through death. Hebrews 10:5 says it this way: *Therefore, when He comes into the world, He says, 'Sacrifice and offering You have not desired, but a body You have prepared for Me.'"* In other words, Jesus came to offer Himself, His own physical body, as the ultimate sacrifice that would pay for the sins of the world – your sin and my sin.

Jesus came in a body also to create a new body of believers. In Him, all those who believe become part of His Spiritual body. This body is also called the church, and is made up of many members, each doing its part so that the whole body functions correctly. Romans 12:4-5 explains this when it says *For just as we have many members in one body and all the members do not have the same function, so we, who are many, are one body in Christ, and individually members of one another.*

Jesus came in a body to show us that God desired to dwell with us and in us. Jesus' very existence proves that the God of the universe inhabits human flesh, giving us confidence that His Spirit does indeed take up residence in us, a gift He promises to those who believe in Him.

Live It Out

The manger reminds us that as the people of God, we are a family, but we are also a body. Jesus humbled Himself to become like us, so that we could become like Him. We have life – eternal life – because we are connected to the source of life, Christ.

Jesus' life in a human body was for a limited time; when He had accomplished salvation, He returned to heaven in a glorified body. The good news is that our physical life will end one day too, and those who are part of His body will spend eternity with Him.

Ephesians 1:22-23 – *And He [God] put all things in subjection under His [Jesus] feet, and gave Him as head over all things to the church, which is His body, the fullness of Him who fills all in all.*

PRAY TODAY
Dear Jesus, The concept of a body is easy for us to understand. What's harder to believe is that You became human to redeem us. But we must believe this if we want to spend eternity with You. Thank You for not just telling us what we must do (Your commandments), which You knew we would fail at keeping, but for coming to be with us. You made Yourself like us to do for us what we could not do for ourselves. Help us to believe and live in this truth. Amen.

Take It In

And behold, you [Mary] will conceive in your womb and bear a son, and you shall name Him Jesus. He will be great and will be called the Son of the Most High; and the Lord God will give Him the throne of His father David; and He will reign over the house of Jacob forever, and His kingdom will have no end. (Luke 1:31-33)

Now having been questioned by the Pharisees, as to when the kingdom of God was coming, He answered them and said, "The kingdom of God is not coming with signs to be observed; nor will they say, 'Look, here it is!' or 'There it is!' For behold, the kingdom of God is in your midst. (Luke 17:20-21)

Think It Through

So far, we've seen that Jesus came to make the people of God a family, and a body (called the church). But there's another description of Christ-followers that we don't think much about in our American culture. It is the concept of a kingdom.

The manger is that piece of the Christmas story that doesn't fit – the reminder that Jesus came humbly, born into physical poverty. The manger stands in stark contrast to what we know to be true: Jesus is the King of Kings, and should have been welcomed in the appropriate fashion. We sing songs about King Jesus, and have no trouble declaring that He is sovereign King over the world, but do we see ourselves as members and servants of His kingdom? A king must have a kingdom.

Jesus came preaching and teaching the kingdom of God. The Jews thought the promised Messiah would be an earthly king, to rescue them from Rome's rule and restore Israel to its former glory on earth. But the kingdom Jesus spoke of was a spiritual kingdom, comprised of all His followers from eternity past, present and future. The kingdom of God is the kingdom of heaven, and His realm of dominion, power, and authority is the hearts of men and women who believe.

Live It Out

Jesus came to declare the kingdom of God is here. He purchased His kingdom when He willingly laid down His life on the cross, and He claimed authority over His kingdom when He rose from the grave. He takes up residence in His kingdom every time someone comes to faith by believing in Him, and He dwells in the hearts of those who belong to His kingdom.

Today, the kingdom of God is not a physical place, but a spiritual entity made up of believers all around the world. Scripture teaches that God has allowed our enemy, Satan, a measure of freedom on earth, until He returns to gather the citizens of His kingdom to heaven. In that day, there will be an accounting of our hearts, to reveal those who belong to the kingdom of God, and expose those who don't.

Is Jesus *your* king? Are you part of the kingdom of God? Will you spend eternity in the kingdom of heaven? The manger cries out for us to recognize the King of Kings sleeping inside, and invites us into His kingdom.

John 18:36 - *Jesus answered, "My kingdom is not of this world. If My kingdom were of this world, then My servants would be fighting so that I would not be handed over to the Jews; but as it is, My kingdom is not of this realm."*

PRAY TODAY
Dear Jesus, Dear King Jesus! To recognize You as King causes us to face the most difficult part of ourselves – our pride. We don't like to surrender. We want to be self-sufficient, and rule our own lives as we see fit. We are blinded to the glorious realities of Your kingdom, deceived to believe that life is better when we are in charge. The truth is You are a good and loving King, who laid down Your life for us. Help us to see You for who You are, and surrender our lives to become part of Your kingdom. And teach us what it means to live as citizens of the kingdom of God in a world that doesn't recognize our great King. Amen.

Day Twenty-Nine

Take It In
But now apart from the Law the righteousness of God has been manifested, being witnessed by the Law and the Prophets, even the righteousness of God through faith in Jesus Christ for all those who believe; for there is no distinction; for all have sinned and fall short of the glory of God, being justified as a gift by His grace through the redemption which is in Christ Jesus. (Romans 3:21-24)

Think It Through
Have you ever thought about why we give gifts at Christmas? The world recognizes Santa as the central figure in the "holiday" celebrations, but the reality is, Christmas is about Christ. The word Christmas itself means "Christ-mass", a worship celebration of Christ. "Holiday" comes from "holy day." And the gifts? We are celebrating the greatest gift of all: salvation for

mankind through Christ. We give gifts because as the people of God, we are a people of *grace* – the gift of God's favor and delight.

A gift is not a gift unless it is given freely, offered unconditionally, and given without merit. If we receive a gift because we did something to earn it, it is a reward, or payment. We receive the benefit of a gift, because *someone else* paid the price to obtain it for us.

Salvation in Christ is a gift, and cannot be earned. God does not weigh our good deeds and bad deeds against each other in the hope that good will win out. No one earns salvation. No one earns heaven.

God's gift of His Son is offered to us, a gift of grace. As we examine this gift, this Child in the manger, we see grace for our past: mercy and forgiveness for our sins; we see grace for today: power for living a holy and meaningful life; and grace for our future: the hope of heaven. How do we obtain this gift? We open our hands (our lives) and take what is offered by faith in the Son of God. No strings attached. Grace.

Live It Out

As people of grace, we live the rest of our lives receiving the blessing and bounty of this gift of God's Son. We are *given* the Spirit of Christ, who indwells us, equipping us to carry out the good works God has planned for us. We are *given* understanding of His Word to guide and comfort us. We are *given* power over sin's temptations. We are *given* a love and compassion for others. No longer do we strive to be good enough to get into heaven. We are freely accepted in Christ – God's gift, by grace through faith.

One other thought. Gifts are given to express love. No one offers a gift because they hate someone. This baby, this Child in the manger is God saying to us, "I love you, and I want to spend eternity with you." How can we not accept such a gift from someone who loves us enough to give us His own Son?

I often wonder why people choose to reject Jesus, but still celebrate Christmas. What meaning could it have, if we fail to recognize the greatest gift of all? The manger reminds us that Christmas is about Christ. It is the picture of grace, the unearned, unequalled and unending favor of God. Are you part of the people of grace? Have you opened the gift?

1 John 4:9-10 – *By this the love of God was manifested in us, that God has sent His only begotten Son into the world so that we might live through Him. In this is love, not that we loved God, but that He loved us and sent His Son to be the propitiation for our sins.*

61

Ephesians 2:8-9 – *For by grace you have been saved through faith; and that not of yourselves, it is the gift of God; not as a result of works, so that no one may boast.*

PRAY TODAY
Dear Jesus, We are all recipients of Your grace and mercy, even before we believe in You. You give us life. You sustain our world. And You continually call us to Yourself in a hundred different ways, whispering of Your grace and love through circumstances, people and the world You created. You love because it's Your nature to love, and Your grace spills over on us every day. Thank You for the gift of Your Son, Jesus. Help us all to see Christmas for what it really is – and to celebrate it by accepting Your offer of grace. Amen.

Day Thirty

Take It In

Jesus spoke these things; and lifting up His eyes to heaven, He said, "Father, the hour has come; glorify Your Son, that the Son may glorify You." … "O righteous Father, although the world has not known You, yet I have known You; and these have known that You sent Me; and I have made Your name known to them, and will make it known, so that the love with which You loved Me may be in them, and I in them." (John 17:1,25-26)

Now to Him who is able to do far more abundantly beyond all that we ask or think, according to the power that works within us, to Him be the glory in the church and in Christ Jesus to all generations forever and ever. Amen. (Ephesians 3:20-21)

Think It Through

Consider Jesus' life from a purely earthly perspective. He was born in a stable with a feeding trough for a cradle, grew up in a small, obscure village as a child born out of wedlock, had an extremely short adult career as a Jewish rabbi with followers who praised Him one day and shouted for His death the next, and ended His life by crucifixion. We would not describe this as a "glorious" life. Yet Jesus prays at the hour of His death, for God to glorify Him, so that He could glorify God.

The word "glorify" (Greek word *doxazo*) means to cause the dignity and worth of some person or thing to become manifest and acknowledged. When Jesus is glorified, His innate glory, His worth, His value, is brought to light. As He was born, lived, died, and rose again, He disclosed the worth and glory and majesty of God. His very life *revealed* God; or to say it another way,

God *revealed Himself* in Christ Jesus. Hebrews 1:3, speaking of Jesus, says *He is the radiance of His [God's] glory and the exact representation of His nature.*

Jesus begins His prayer in John 17 asking His Father to glorify Him, so that He could in turn glorify His Father. At the end of the chapter, He tells us *how* God is glorified: God's **name** is made known, and His **love** is made real. Jesus' prayer in this chapter expresses a longing for those who believe in Him to experience the same relationship that He has with His Father. He asks that His followers know God intimately, be filled with joy, be sanctified in truth, and be protected from evil. When this happens, Jesus' work is accomplished, and God is glorified.

Live It Out

The people of the manger, those who believe, are to carry on this task of glorifying God, through Christ in us. In a sense, Jesus left us His legacy – His purpose. He was sent to reveal God to us, and in calling us to Himself, we become part of His work – to make His name and His great love for men known to the world.

As Jesus glorified His Father, so we, as the church, the body of Christ, are to glorify Jesus. We are to *bring to light* His worth, His majesty, His value, and His power. Do you know His name? Have you experienced His love? Glorify God.

John 17:22-23 – *The glory which You have given Me I have given to them, that they may be one, just as We are one; I in them and You in Me, that they may be perfected in unity, so that the world may know that You sent Me, and loved them, even as You have loved Me.*

PRAY TODAY
Dear Jesus, We marvel at Your prayer for us in John 17. Hours before Your death, You were talking to Your Father about those who would believe. As You faced the hardest part of Your earthly journey in human flesh, the physical pain of crucifixion and the spiritual burden of carrying all the sins of mankind to the cross, You were looking to the future. Your desire for us to experience the same love of the Father carried You to the cross. When we look at the manger, we are reminded that You came to glorify God by bringing men to salvation. Help us to carry out this same great work that You left for us to do – to make Your name and Your love known to all. Amen.

Take It In

There came a man sent from God, whose name was John. He came as a witness, to testify about the Light, so that all might believe through him. ... The next day he saw Jesus coming to him and said, "Behold the Lamb of God who takes away the sin of the world! ... I myself have seen, and have testified that this is the Son of God." (John 1:6-7, 29, 34)

Think It Through

John the Baptist is not usually a character included in our nativity scene, but he should be! After all, he was a part of Jesus' life from the very beginning – even before Jesus was born – and his own birth was surrounded by supernatural events. Luke 1 gives us the details. His parents were advanced in age, never having children. His father, a priest, was visited in the temple by an angel who promised him they would have a son named John who would go as a forerunner to call Israel to repentance and prepare the way for the Lord.

John was intimately connected to his cousin, Jesus. While six months pregnant, his mother, Elizabeth, was visited by her young relative, Mary, who was already carrying Jesus. When Mary greeted Elizabeth, John leaped in the womb, and his mother was filled with the Holy Spirit, just as the angel had promised his father that the baby would be filled with the Holy Spirit *while yet in his mother's womb.* These two women knew from the beginning that the two babies they carried would be part of each other's lives in a way that would affect history.

John did indeed grow up and began to preach repentance to the nation. When Jesus began His ministry at age thirty, his cousin was there to point Him out and proclaim, "This is the Son of God!" John became Jesus' most vocal witness, encouraging his own disciples to follow Him. He spent his short ministry unashamedly declaring the kingdom of God, and eventually lost his life for boldly confronting Herod's sinful behavior.

Live It Out

To John the Baptist, the Child in the manger was most assuredly the promised Messiah. He knew the stories of their unusual births, and I'm confident that his mother, Elizabeth, and his relative, Mary, got together many times to talk about these events and encourage each other in raising these two special boys into the men of purpose they became.

As a person impacted by the manger, John was a true *martys* (Greek word for "witness" as used in Acts 1:8). This same word gives us our word "martyr" – one who gives his life for a cause he believes in. John's example inspires us to be people who proclaim the truth about who this Child in the manger really is – the Lamb of God, who takes away the sin of the world! Are you like John, proclaiming Jesus? Or do you need to hear John's message, the voice of one crying in the wilderness, "Make straight the way of the Lord."

John 3:27-28, 36 – *John answered and said, "A man can receive nothing unless it has been given him from heaven. You yourselves are my witnesses that I said, 'I am not the Christ,' but, 'I have been sent ahead of Him.' ... He who believes in the Son has eternal life, but he who does not obey the Son will not see life, but the wrath of God abides on him."*

PRAY TODAY
Dear Jesus, Your earthly cousin John had a very special relationship with You. He knew You as a child, and I believe You were there as he discovered the call of God on his life. He believed in You, and was not ashamed to tell the world, even to losing his life for speaking the truth about sin. We can learn a lot from John the Baptist, and ask You to make us into mighty witnesses of the power of God in our own lives. John testified to what He knew: You are the Son of God who takes away our sin. Help us to be bold like Him, and lead others to You. Amen.

The Person of the Manger
Day 32-40

Living in light of the manger starts with understanding its *purpose*,
and the *promises* God fulfilled in sending His Son.
In the *presence* of the manger, we learn things about
ourselves, and how God wants to have a relationship with us.
As we begin to understand God's great gift of love and mercy,
we must respond with a *passion* – accept or reject.
Passionate acceptance leads us to apprehend the *power* the manger
has to change our lives, and make us the *people* of God,
people who worship the *person* of the manger.

When Jesus as born, everyone had an idea of who He was, and who He
would become. But we don't have to wonder anymore. He tells us plainly:
I am.

The *person* of the manger is the great *I AM*, come to reveal God to us.

Take It In

*So they said to Him, "What then do You do for a sign, so that we may see, and believe You? What work do You perform? Our fathers ate the manna in the wilderness; as it is written, 'He gave them bread out of heaven to eat.'" Jesus then said to them, "Truly, truly, I say to you, it is not Moses who has given you the bread out of heaven, but it is My Father who gives you the true bread out of heaven. For the bread of God is that which comes down out of heaven, and gives life to the world." ... Jesus said to them, "**I am the bread of life**; he who comes to Me will not hunger, and he who believes in Me will never thirst." (John 6:30-33,35)*

Think It Through

The context of these verses is a miracle. Jesus had just fed the five thousand with five loaves and two fish. Counting women and children, scholars estimate there were upwards of twenty thousand that ate! The crowds were amazed, and they had followed Jesus to the other side of the sea of Galilee. They sought Him for two reasons. Jesus had satisfied their physical hunger, and He had done it in a supernatural way. They wanted more. Hence their demand: *Perform for us!* They challenged Jesus to do something as astonishing as the bread of heaven, the manna, that was provided to their ancestors in the wilderness.

The people wanted relief from their work. Life was difficult, and to receive free bread was desirable. Jesus challenges the people to stop working for physical food which only sustains the body for a time, and eventually ends in death. Rather, we should work for that which gives eternal life – the *bread of life.* And how do we work for this bread? We come to Him in hunger, and we believe (John 6:29).

Manna was a gift to the wandering Israelites. It appeared each morning on the ground. God provided it, but for it to sustain them, they had to go out and collect it. By faith, they had to believe it would nourish them and provide what they needed to live. They had to take it into their bodies. Jesus uses this same terminology at the end of John 6, telling the Jews that He will give His flesh, His body, as the living bread, and that they must eat His flesh and drink His blood to gain eternal life. Of course, they were offended that He spoke this way, because they missed the spiritual reality He intended. They were blind to the truth.

Live It Out

As the Bread of Life, Jesus alone sustains us and gives us eternal life. Physical bread provides for our flesh; Jesus provides life to our spirit. Also, we must receive Him into our life by faith. Believing means more than an intellectual assent that God is real, and Jesus came and died. When we eat bread, it becomes part of us; we can no longer separate ourselves from it. To believe is to give our lives over to Christ so that He now lives in us. We no longer exist except by the power of the Spirit who indwells us. Jesus said it this way: *We abide in Him, and He abides in us* (John 6:56).

The Jews sought Jesus to provide for their physical needs, and to entertain them by His miracles. We must ask ourselves what we are looking for when we seek after God. Do we just want a God that performs for us, giving us what we want? Jesus came to give us abundant life now, and eternal life forever. We must choose if we will accept what He provided to sustain our spiritual life, or be deceived by what gratifies our flesh, but leads to death. How have you responded to His offer of the *bread of life*?

Galatians 2:20 - *I have been crucified with Christ; and it is no longer I who live, but Christ lives in me; and the life which I now live in the flesh I live by faith in the Son of God, who loved me and gave Himself up for me.*

PRAY TODAY
Dear Jesus, By calling Yourself the Bread of Life, we can understand more of our relationship with You. You sustain us, and give us life. You come to live in us, as we take You by faith, and receive You. You now live Your life in us, giving us the abundant life of joy, peace, and purpose what You always desired us to have. And when this life is over, we get to spend eternity with You. Thank You for offering Yourself up as the Bread of Life. Forgive us when we believe life comes from the empty substitutes the world offers, and teach us to find our life in You. Amen.

Day Thirty-Three: Jesus Shines In Our Darkness

Take It In

*Then Jesus again spoke to them, saying, "**I am the Light of the world**; he who follows Me will not walk in the darkness, but will have the Light of life." (John 8:12)*

I have come as Light into the world, so that everyone who believes in Me will not remain in darkness. (John 12:46)

Think It Through

Have you ever seen an illustration of the nativity scene in which there is an ethereal glow coming from the manger? Or the manger itself is bathed in a stream of light coming from the heavens? The artist is telling us something that is biblical and true – Jesus came into our world to bring light. In fact, He calls Himself *the Light of the world.*

Light is the opposite of darkness. Some scientists say that darkness does not exist at all; it is simply the absence of light. Jesus came to shine the glory of God in our world of darkness, literally and spiritually. Spiritual darkness is the absence of the knowledge of God. Our minds and hearts are darkened, unaware of God and fully convinced that we are right (Romans 1).

Just as our eyes adjust to a darkened room, our fallen human nature adjusts to the darkness of sin and evil. Without the Light of Christ to expose the darkness, we begin to believe that we are seeing correctly. Proverbs 4:19 says it this way: *The way of the wicked is like darkness; they do not know over what they stumble.* You've experienced this, perhaps trying to convince someone to believe what they can't see, when it seems so obvious to you.

Trying to understand the truth of salvation is often like standing at the door of a dark room, straining to see what is inside. The darker it is behind and around you, the less you can see. If there is some light, you may be able to see shapes, but you cannot truly know what is in the room. If, however, you step across the threshold, the light comes on in the room, and everything is clearly seen. This is the moment of belief, of surrender to Christ. By faith, we step out of darkness and into the Light.

Live It Out

Many of us had lots of light around us as we stood at the door to salvation. Perhaps we attended church as a child, or had a grandmother who told us the Bible stories. We had believing parents, siblings, or friends, who shared truth with us. It was a simple step for us to believe, as Jesus enlightened us, showing us our sin and inviting us in. Others have had so much light, we assume we are living in the light, yet have never stepped across the threshold of true, saving faith. We are in darkness, but do not know it.

Still, others of us have lived in darkness our whole lives, without any godly influence or spiritual truth. Surrounded by darkness, we look into salvation and struggle to understand. Jesus comes near to us, and opens our eyes to the Light. He exposes our sin, and whispers His grace and love and mercy. He shines the light, and shows us the way to salvation.

This tiny baby in the manger came to be the Light of our world. His pushes back the darkness, and invites us to live in the glorious Light of His presence. Are you living in darkness, or in Light? Are your eyes deceived, stumbling over things you cannot understand? Ask Jesus to shine on your soul and enlighten your heart to see Him for who He is – the Light of the world.

Colossians 1:12-13 – *Giving thanks to the Father, who has qualified us to share in the inheritance of the saints in Light. For He rescued us from the domain of darkness, and transferred us to the kingdom of His beloved Son.*

PRAY TODAY
Dear Jesus, Thank You for coming into our world to shine the Light. You expose what is evil and wicked and sinful, and without You to enlighten our hearts, we would go on believing that we have life figured out, and die in our sins. As Your children, You call us to be light in this world, shining examples of who You are, by walking in light and avoiding the darkness of sin. Help us to shine Your light to others. And if we do not know You yet, give us the faith to step across the threshold to salvation, believing in You. Amen.

Day Thirty-Four: Jesus Shows Us The Way

Take It In
*"Do not let your hearts be troubled; believe in God, believe also in Me. In My Father's house are many dwelling places; if it were not so, I would have told you; for I go to prepare a place for you. If I go and prepare a place for you, I will come again and receive you to Myself, that where I am, there you may be also. And you know the way where I am going. Thomas said to Him, "Lord, we do not know where You are going, how do we know the way?" Jesus said to him, "**I am the way, and the truth, and the life**; no one comes to the Father but through Me." (John 14:1-6)*

Think It Through
The first part of John 14 contains the encouraging words we all love: Jesus has gone to heaven to prepare us a place, and is coming back to take us there. We ALL love those words...the promise of heaven. But consider the context of Jesus' words of promise. In response to Peter's declaration that he would remain loyal even being willing to die for Him, Jesus warns Peter that he will deny Him three times before the rooster crows! What? Peter would deny Him, turn His back on Jesus, and out of fear, be unable to admit He even knows Him ... and Jesus, knowing this will happen, tells him, "Don't let your heart be troubled ... believe in Me!"

Our acceptance in Christ is based on Jesus' determination to have us. It is due to His claim on us, not our ability to remain true and faithful. When we disappoint ourselves by failing to be faithful to Him, Jesus Himself tells us, "Don't worry. I've got you. Believe in Me (not yourself!). I'm still coming back to get you, because I've already started working on your new home."

Note Jesus' bold claim: "I am the way, and the truth, and the life; no one comes to the Father but through Me." There is no other way to God, to heaven, and to eternal life, except through Jesus. We might say Jesus shows us the way to God. No...Jesus *is* the way to God.

Live It Out

Jesus is the **way**, because He alone paid our sin debt. Our good works, our kind acts of compassion, and concern for our fellow man are all noble and virtuous, and evidence that we are created in the image of God. But they do not purchase our salvation. *For all of us have become like one who is unclean, and all our righteous deeds are like a filthy garment; and all of us wither like a leaf, and our iniquities, like the wind, take us away.* (Isaiah 64:6)

Jesus is the **truth**, because He alone is willing to reveal our sin that keeps us from God. He does not give us false hope that we can choose our own path if we believe hard enough. *For the Law was given through Moses; grace and truth were realized through Jesus Christ.* (John 1:17)

Jesus is the **life**, because He alone is Creator, the giver of life. He gave us physical life, knitting us together in our mother's womb. He offers abundant life, indwelling believers through His Spirit and living in and through us. And He promises eternal life, heaven, where we will have joy forever in the presence of God. *Truly, truly, I say to you, he who hears My word, and believes Him who sent Me, has eternal life, and does not come into judgment, but has passed out of death into life.* (John 5:24)

This is the Child of the manger. Are you following the way? Have you believed the truth? Do you possess eternal life?

PRAY TODAY
Dear Jesus, Thank You for not only showing us the way to God, but becoming the way. Some people might think that it's rather unfair to only have one way to God, but the reality is that it is the ultimate in justice and fairness. All are equal before You, and You desire all men to come. You are the most fair God of all, because You provided the way. Other religions tell us how we can get to heaven by fulfilling certain requirements. Instead, You fulfilled all the requirements for us – we simply have to take You at Your word and believe.

Help us, as you did for doubting Thomas, to believe in You. And we when we fail You like Peter, remind us that You have already forgiven us. Amen.

Day Thirty-Five: Jesus Shepherds Us

Take It In
I am the good shepherd; the good shepherd lays down His life for the sheep. He who is a hired hand, and not a shepherd, who is not the owner of the sheep, sees the wolf coming, and leaves the sheep and flees, and the wolf snatches them and scatters them. He flees because he is a hired hand and is not concerned about the sheep. I am the good shepherd, and I know My own and My own know Me, even as the Father knows Me and I know the Father; and I lay down My life for the sheep. (John 10:11-15)

Think It Through
I find it amazing that when God created sheep He did so, knowing that this gentle, stubborn, foolish creature would become a symbol of His people, and that His Son would be born on earth as a human child and grow up to call Himself **the Good Shepherd.** He created this unique animal with all its character traits knowing it would help us understand ourselves and our relationship with Holy God.

The people of the Old Testament and in Jesus' day were very familiar with shepherds and sheep. When Isaiah spoke of *going astray like sheep*, they recognized their own tendencies to wander away from God (Isaiah 53:6). When Jesus told a parable of a shepherd searching for *one lost sheep*, they understood God's passion for the man or woman searching for truth (Matthew 18:12). And when He called Himself the *Good Shepherd*, they could grasp His commitment to His people.

Jesus identified two specific actions that qualified Him as **the Good Shepherd.** First, He was willing to lay down His life for His sheep. Unlike the hired man, who was concerned about preserving his own life, Jesus was not only *willing* to lay down His life, He *did* lay it down. Second, He knows His sheep, and they know Him. Sheep follow their shepherd's voice, because he has spent time with them. He has pulled them out of difficulties, cared for their wounds, carried them as lambs, talked to them, and led them to pasture. He knows them intimately, and they trust him implicitly. In the same way, Jesus knows His own – those who belong to Him now, and those who will belong to Him.

Live It Out

The wolf comes for two reasons: to snatch and to scatter. In other words, the enemy desires to keep us away from the shepherd, and to destroy our lives. Sheep are stubborn, often determined to go their own way despite the danger. Sheep are foolish, straying too far. Sheep cannot survive without the shepherd. Our enemy knows this, and desires to keep us from trusting the Good Shepherd.

On that first Christmas morning, a group of shepherds knelt at the foot of the manger to worship **the Good Shepherd**, sent from God. Jesus came to gather His sheep into the fold. He came to claim His own, to call them to Himself and to lay down His life for them. Have you heard the voice of your shepherd?

Psalm 100:3 - *Know that the Lord Himself is God; it is He who has made us, and not we ourselves; we are His people and the sheep of His pasture.*

PRAY TODAY
Dear Jesus, I love the image of the Good Shepherd who tenderly cares for the sheep. I admit that sometimes I am stubborn and willful, and get myself into predicaments. Thank You for coming to my rescue many times, and for loving me and caring for me as Your own. Thank You most of all for laying down Your life for me. You did what was necessary to protect and save us from sin, ourselves, and the enemy of our soul, because You are our good good Shepherd. Thank You for loving us that much. Amen.

Day Thirty-Six: Jesus Secures Our Eternal Life

Take It In

*Jesus said to her, "**I am the resurrection and the life**; he who believes in Me will live even if he dies, and everyone who lives and believes in Me will never die. Do you believe this?" (John 11:25-26)*

These will go away into eternal punishment, but the righteous into eternal life. (Matthew 25:46)

Think It Through

The Bible teaches that every soul will live eternally. We are a unique creation of God, made of body, soul and spirit. The first man, Adam, was brought to life when God breathed into him the breath of life, and he became a living being. Adam's soul and spirit were alive, and were contained in a physical, human body that should have lived forever. Adam sinned, however, and his spirit life, the connection to His creator, was shattered. His soul (his mind, will, emotions, personality, intellect) lived on in a physical body that would now die (*the wages of sin is death*). Instead of finding his joy and purpose and life in God, man now looks to his own soul. Sin stole our spirit life, mortally wounded our physical life, and corrupted our soul to look to self rather than God.

Jesus came to fix this. *I am the resurrection* – Jesus has power to raise our physical bodies up from the grave and return them to their glorious, eternal state. *I am the life* – Jesus has power to heal our broken spirit; our connection to God can be restored.

With or without Jesus, our souls will live for eternity. All of us know this, deep down. We cannot imagine ourselves not existing. We cannot comprehend "nothingness" even if we say we believe that we will cease to be when we die. In our heart of hearts, we know there is something after death. The Bible tells us what eternity will be for those who do not believe Jesus' words or accept His grace and mercy, but we don't like to talk about it. It's unpleasant, scary. We'd rather not think about our souls living for eternity in place of darkness, evil, and torment – a place called hell.

Live It Out

Everything about this tiny baby in the manger speaks of good news. The angel said it: *I bring you good news of great joy which will be for all the people* (Luke 2:10). What is the good news? **It is that Jesus has come to be our resurrection and our life.** God's heart breaks for the souls He has created that are separated from Him. He longs to give us back the hope of new, physical bodies that will live forever, and bring to life our spirit to commune with Him. His desire is redemption for the souls of men – your soul, and mine.

The hope of resurrection and eternal life is good news because we know the bad news. Consider your physical body. Is it improving daily? Growing stronger, younger? Of course not; we are all slowing dying (some of us faster than others), giving evidence that truly death has come into our world. The bad news is, we are dying physically, and are spiritually dead. But Jesus has come – *the resurrection and the life!* Oh, my friend, do you believe?

John 5:24 - *Truly, truly, I say to you, he who hears My word, and believes Him who sent Me, has eternal life, and does not come into judgment, but has passed out of death into life.*

PRAY TODAY

Dear Jesus, Why do we refuse to believe the good news? Are we too skeptical? Too stubborn? Or is it just too good to be true? You came to bring life – to give us the gift of eternity in heaven, and to resurrect our physical bodies to be like Your glorified body. Open our eyes to see the love and grace and mercy and life that You came to give us. And as we see You and believe and accept who You are, recognizing our desperate need for forgiveness and redemption, help us to live our lives in a way that proclaims You as our resurrection and our life. Amen.

Day Thirty-Seven: Jesus Stays With Us

Take It In

I am the true vine, and My Father is the vinedresser. ... Abide in Me, and I in you. As the branch cannot bear fruit of itself unless it abides in the vine, so neither can you unless you abide in Me. I am the vine, you are the branches; he who abides in Me and I in him, he bears much fruit, for apart from Me you can do nothing. (John 15:1,3-4)

Think It Through

When Jesus spoke these words, He was most likely walking through grape vines on His way to the Garden of Gethsemane. In less than 24 hours He would be hanging on a cross, and He used the last minutes with His disciples to communicate some very important truths. As was His habit, He used a physical illustration to convey a spiritual lesson.

The vine is the source of life in a vineyard. Unless it is connected to the vine, the branch cannot produce fruit. It must have the life which flows from the vine. If the branch is separated, it is useless, good only to be burned or thrown away. The disciples would have to remain (abide) in Christ even after He died, was resurrected, and returned to heaven, if they were to continue following Him. How would this be possible?

The disciples, and all believers who came after them, would abide in Christ because **He would abide in them.** Jesus promised to send the Holy Spirit to be with them forever: *He abides with you and will be in you.* (John 14:16-17). Here is what separates Christianity from every other religion. Spiritual life is not achieved by a prescribed set of good works, or levels of personal enlightenment. It is given as a gift, when God's Spirit comes to abide in us. As many have said, following Jesus is not a religion; it is a relationship.

Live It Out

Scripture gives us many practical evidences that God's Spirit does truly indwell (abide in) the believer. We bear fruit, we keep His commands, we are filled with joy, we love one another, we see answers to prayer, we have a hatred of sin, we experience unexplainable peace in the midst of hardship, and we can forgive when wronged. But there is one primary evidence, without which we cannot claim that we belong to Him. John says it this way: *Whoever confesses that Jesus is the Son of God, God abides in him and he in God.* (1 John 4:15).

Without recognizing Jesus as who He claims to be, the Son of God, we cannot abide in Him, nor does He abide in us. Jesus did not come only to be loved and worshipped as a baby in a manger. He came to reveal Himself as the One True God, Savior, Lord and Master of our lives. He did not come just to visit; He came to indwell and abide in His followers. He came to stay.

Has He come to you? Do you believe that He is the Son of God? Are you abiding in Him?

1 John 4:12-13 – *No one has seen God at any time; if we love one another, God abides in us, and His love is perfected in us. By this we know that we abide in Him and He in us, because He has given us of His Spirit.*

PRAY TODAY
Dear Jesus, Thank You that You did not come just to visit our world and leave us on our own to try to follow You. You sent Your Spirit to indwell every person who surrenders their life to You in faith, so that You could abide in us and we could abide in You. What an amazing thing – God wants to stay with us! Thank You for loving us that much. Teach us to walk in awareness of Your presence, abiding in You. Amen.

Day Thirty-Eight: Jesus Summons Us

Take It In

*So Jesus said to them again, "Truly, truly, I say to you, **I am the door of the sheep.** All who came before Me are thieves and robbers, but the sheep did not hear them. **I am the door**; if anyone enters through Me, he will be saved, and will go in and out and find pasture. The thief comes only to steal and kill and destroy; I came that they may have life, and have it abundantly." (John 10:7-10)*

Think It Through

Here Jesus refers to Himself as **the door of the sheep.** The door (or gate) was the place the shepherd lay each night after all the sheep were safely in the fold. The shepherd knew each sheep personally, and they came to the fold where their shepherd waited for them to enter. They had to come through him to find rest, just as we come through Jesus to find rest for our souls.

Jesus' claim is clear and bold. The way to salvation is only through Him, **the door.** To attempt to come to God in any other way is to be a thief and a robber. This is a hard saying, for many of us desire to gain heaven and God's approval in other ways – good and thoughtful ways that appear to be worthwhile and honorable. Yet Jesus' words confront us to consider the truth that He is the only door.

Jesus' words warn us that others are thieves and robbers who desire to steal, kill and destroy the sheep. Who are these thieves and robbers? They are false shepherds, those who would tell us there are other ways to heaven.

Jesus Himself refers to the way to heaven as *narrow.* We have no trouble understanding and accepting this concept of "one way" in every part of our life. If we buy a plane ticket to Atlanta, we must go through the gate listed on our boarding pass. We must sit in the seat number assigned, and we must be sitting in the right airplane! The pilot must land on the *narrow* runway. We cannot get to Atlanta by simply walking up to any gate, any plane, and *believing with all our heart* that the plane of our choosing will get us to our destination. It's a very *narrow* way to travel, just as the road to salvation is narrow.

Live It Out

We hear often, "all roads lead to God." But this is not even logical. Recently my husband and I were asked to speak in a church that was located an hour and half from our home. As we left our neighborhood, we had to make the decision which road to take. Because we had directions, we took the correct road. By the logic of "all roads lead to God," we should have been able to simply turn any way we wished, and arrive safely at our destination just by believing it to be the right road. Of course, this is foolish. Just because we believe something doesn't make it true. And not believing doesn't make it *not true.*

The beauty and blessing of the manger is that the door to heaven and eternal life is open. Jesus has made the way. He Himself is the door, providing access to God. He invites all to enter: *Behold, I stand at the door and knock; if anyone hears My voice and opens the door, I will come in to him and will dine with him, and he with Me. (Revelation 3:20)*

Picture it this way. Jesus opened the door to heaven, and stepped into our world as a tiny baby. He accomplished salvation through the cross and resurrection, and returned to heaven, leaving the door open for us to follow. The light is on, and the table is set, but we must accept His invitation.

Matthew 7:13-14 – *Enter through the narrow gate; for the gate is wide and the way is broad that leads to destruction, and there are many who enter through it. For the gate is small and the way is narrow that leads to life, and there are few who find it.*

PRAY TODAY
Dear Jesus, Thank You for opening the door to heaven for us. Thank You for **being** *the door, the way to salvation. Help us to surrender our high opinions of ourselves, and accept the gift of the open door to salvation. You welcome us, inviting us to spend eternity with You, and all You ask is that we come believing. Thank You for showing us the way. Amen.*

Day Thirty-Nine: Jesus Is Superior

Take It In
Then Moses said to God, "Behold, I am going to the sons of Israel, and I will say to them, 'The God of your fathers has sent me to you.' Now they may say to me, 'What is His name?' What shall I say to them?" God said to Moses, "I AM WHO I AM;" and He said, "Thus you shall say to the sons of Israel, 'I AM has sent me to you.'" God, furthermore, said to Moses, "Thus you shall say to the sons of Israel, 'The Lord, the God of your fathers, the God of Abraham, the God of Isaac, and the God of Jacob, has sent me to you.' This is My name forever, and this is My memorial-name to all generations." (Exodus 3:13-15)

So the Jews said to Him, "You are not yet fifty years old, and have You seen Abraham?" Jesus said to them, "Truly, truly, I say to you, before Abraham was born, I am." Therefore they picked up stones to throw at Him, but Jesus hid Himself and went out of the temple. (John 8:57-59)

Think It Through

Moses' encounter with God in Exodus 3 describes a very unusual event. God spoke out of a burning bush – a bush that was on fire, but was not consumed. It was here that Moses received his marching orders, literally, to lead the nation of Israel out of Egypt's captivity. God would rescue them, but He would use Moses to do it.

Moses is one of the most revered prophets in the Jewish faith, along with Abraham. To claim not only equality, but superiority, over these two forefathers was tantamount to blasphemy. This was exactly what Jesus did when He made His claim to exist before Abraham, using God's special name, *I AM.* Jesus was not being vague; the Jews understood exactly what He meant, as we see by their reaction: they were ready to stone Him. Jesus claimed not only to be sent from God, He declared that He was God – the God of the Old Testament, *I AM.*

What did God mean by the name? The Hebrew phrase is *hayah hayah.* The word *hayah* is to be, or to exist. God is, because He is. He is not a result of anything; He simply exists because He is. The phrase "I am" is closely related to God's revealed name of Jehovah – the self-existent One. He has no beginning, no end, no cause of becoming. He has always been, and will always be. This is the Triune God, one God, revealed in three Persons – Father, Son and Spirit.

Live It Out

The Jews today still do not accept Jesus as the promised Messiah. He stood in front of them, declaring Himself to be who they were looking for, but they were blinded by their own idea of what the Messiah would look like and how they thought He would act. They were looking for a king, and Jesus came as a servant. They were looking to be rescued from the physical oppression of Rome, and Jesus came to rescue from the spiritual oppression of sin. Jesus revealed Himself by His words and His works, but they still could not believe.

The great **I AM**, Almighty God, is a mystery. He is transcendent, above our world, and beyond understanding, yet revealed Himself in human form so that we could know Him. He is eternally self-existent, revealed in Christ, and present today in Spirit. He is a tiny baby in a manger, a beaten man on a cross, a risen and glorified Savior, and one day, a mighty King returning to take His rightful place in His creation. What is our response to **I AM?** Will we follow Him in obedience as Moses did, or will we pick up stones to throw, and miss the One for whom our soul desires?

John 6:40 – *For this is the will of My Father, that everyone who beholds the Son and believes in Him will have eternal life, and I Myself will raise him up on the last day.*

PRAY TODAY
Dear Jesus, How clearly You revealed Yourself to the people who walked alongside You during Your earthly journey! In the same way today, You do not hide who You are. You reveal Yourself to us every day, through Your creation, through the very life and breath You give us, but because we are not looking for You, or perhaps we have imagined You differently, we do not hear You, or recognize You. You are the self-existent One, the eternal God who created us to worship You. Speak to our hearts, and draw us to You. Open our eyes so that we can recognize the One who loves us and gave Himself for us. Amen.

Day Forty

Take It In
By this the love of God was manifested in us, that God has sent His only begotten Son into the world so that we might live through Him. In this in love, not that we loved God, but that He loved us and sent His Son to be the propitiation for our sins. ... We have seen and testify that the Father has sent the Son to be the Savior of the world. (1 John 4:9-10,14)

At that time the disciples came to Jesus and said, "Who then is greatest in the kingdom of heaven?" And He called a child to Himself and set him before them, and said, "Truly I say to you, unless you are converted and become like children, you will not enter the kingdom of heaven." (Matthew 18:1-3)

Think It Through
Christmas is for children. There's no better picture of the wonder and amazement of child-like faith. *He's like a kid at Christmas* is an accurate statement when our eyes are opened to the real meaning and message of the manger.

1 John 4:14 is the first verse a child memorizes when they enter the AWANA program as a three-year-old. They have no trouble reciting the abbreviated version in typical preschool sing-song fashion: *The Father sent the Son to be the Savior of the world.* I can still hear my own children repeating this, motivated by another sticker in their book. The theological implications escaped them, but as this truth from God's word took root in their heart, they soon came to believe it.

Jesus taught us that to enter the kingdom of heaven, two things must happen: we must be converted, and we must become like children. The Greek word translated as "converted" doesn't denote "changed" as you might think. It is the word *strephō*, and means to "turn around, turn back, or to turn one's self from one's course of conduct, to change one's mind." We are headed one direction, and we change course, and turn to go in the opposite direction. Another word for this in scripture is *repent*.

Why do we need child-like faith to repent? **We must believe what the Bible tells us: there needs to be a change.** We must recognize that our present direction is headed toward destruction and eternal separation of God. Our present circumstances may deceive us, so we must, as a child, believe the truth that we are told – we must turn away from ourselves, and turn to God.

Manifested. Begotten. Propitiation. John uses some big words to explain the simple truth we call the gospel.

*The love of God was **manifested**.* Made known. Revealed. Brought to light. God's love was *manifested* at the manger, when Jesus was born into our world.

*God has sent His only **begotten** Son into the world.* Single of its kind. Only. One commentary says it this way: *Begotten indicates that as the Son of God, Jesus was the sole representative of the Being and character of the One who sent Him.* The message of the manger is the singular, unique Son of God – no other gods will do.

*God sent His Son to be the **propitiation** for our sins.* Appease. Conciliate. Satisfy. God's wrath against sin (your sin, my sin) was *propitiated* by what the Child in the manger would grow up to do.

Live It Out

At the cross, God poured out His wrath on His Son, satisfying our sin debt, so that in Christ, those who believe are brought back into a righteous relationship with God. **This is why child-like faith is imperative.** It's too easy – too unbelievable. Our sin exchanged for Christ's righteousness? There must be a catch. Or is there?

The message of the manger can't be true if we examine it in our human logic. Child-like faith means believing; simply accepting the gift. This is the real meaning of Christmas, and it's offered to you.

John 3:16 – *For God so loved the world, that He gave His only begotten Son, that whoever believes in Him shall not perish, but have eternal life.*

PRAY TODAY

Dear Jesus, On Christmas Day, we celebrate You, whether we realize it or not! We recognize it at Your birthday, the day You were born of a virgin in a small town called Bethlehem – Your entrance into our world. But we know You did not begin Your life there, for You are God, eternally existing, Creator of the world You came to save. Today we give and receive gifts on Christmas Day. Give us child-like faith so that we may we accept the best gift of all – Your salvation – and teach us what it means to live our lives as Your children. Thank You for loving us and showing us the truth. Amen.

Day Forty-One: Now What?

My prayer is that you have been encouraged, challenged, and blessed over the last 40 days. God desires for you to live the abundant life Jesus promised us in John 10:10, and enjoy eternal life with Him forever. If you are already a follower of Jesus, you know this! I hope this journey has reminded you of the miracle of salvation, and caused your relationship with God to deepen and that you will **live in light of the manger.** I encourage you to share the good news of the manger all year round. The Christmas story is not just about one day each year. Every day, you meet people who need to know the truth about Jesus. I pray your journey doesn't end here, but that the truths from God's Word will take root in your life, and bear fruit.

My friend, if you are not a believer, I pray you have heard Him speaking to your heart, and will accept His invitation to eternal life. Here is how you can respond.

Recognize that you are separated from God (admit).
Romans 3:23 - *For all have sinned and come short of the glory of God.*
Be willing to turn from your sin (repent).
1 John 1:9 – *If we confess our sins, He is faithful and righteous to forgive us our sins and to cleanse us from all unrighteousness.*
Believe that Jesus died on the cross and rose from the grave (accept).
Romans 10:9-10 – *That if you confess with your mouth Jesus as Lord, and believe in your heart that God raised Him from the dead; you will be saved; for with the heart a person believes, resulting in righteousness, and with the mouth he confesses, resulting in salvation.*
Invite Jesus in to control your life through the Holy Spirit (receive).
John 1:12 – *But as many as received Him, to them He gave the right to become children of God, even to those who believe in His name.*

What To Pray
Dear Jesus, I recognize that I am separated from You because of my personal sin, and I need Your forgiveness. I believe that You died on the cross to pay the penalty for my sin. I confess my sin and ask You to forgive me. By faith, I turn from my way of life to follow You instead, and accept Your gift of salvation by grace. I ask You to come into my life and transform me. Thank You for saving me and giving me eternal life. Amen.

If you sincerely prayed this prayer and surrendered your life to God, you are now His child. Please share this decision with another believer and ask them to help you get started in how to walk in your new life in Christ. I would love to hear about your decision!

About The Author

Sheila Alewine came to Christ at an early age, growing up in a Baptist church in Western North Carolina. She spent a lot of time in and around church with a mom who worked as the church secretary, so marrying a full-time minister came naturally. She met her husband, Todd, while attending Liberty University in Lynchburg, VA; they married in 1985 and have spent their lives serving God together while raising two daughters.

As a young mom, Sheila fell in love with Bible study when asked to join a Precept study. Throughout the years of raising their daughters, working full-time and serving in ministry, she has loved studying and teaching in the Word. Now at this time of "empty-nest" life, she is enjoying the opportunity to try her hand at writing to encourage other believers.

Sheila and her husband reside in Hendersonville, NC, where they have established *Around The Corner Ministries* to equip and encourage followers of Christ to share the gospel where they live, work and play. They love spending time with their two daughters, sons-in-law, and grandchildren.

***

Want to learn more about sharing the gospel with your neighbors? Our six-week Bible study, **Going Around The Corner**, is perfect for individual or small group study. Visit our website to order your copy!

Also available: **40 Days Of Spiritual Awareness**: **Becoming Aware of How God is Working In and Around You** (Devotional).

Around The Corner Ministries exists to take the gospel to every neighborhood in America. Our mission is to equip followers of Jesus to engage their neighborhoods and communities with the gospel of Jesus Christ.

Around The Corner Ministries is a partner to the local church, designed to teach and train Christ-followers how to share their faith in their neighborhoods, workplaces, and communities. The goal is to grow healthy local churches filled with mature believers who are passionate about the gospel. If you would like more information on how our ministry can partner with your local church, please contact us.

If this devotional has made an impact on your life, please let us know by contacting us through our website **aroundthecornerministries.org**.